Inside the Spaghetti Bowl

FRANK ZACCARI

Copyright © 2011 Frank Zaccari
All rights reserved.

ISBN: 1463650035
ISBN-13: 9781463650032

Dedication:

To our Mother

Carmela Zaccari

1932–2009

And when you remember me:
remember me laughing not crying,
remember me singing not sighing,
remember me living not dying;
or don't remember me at all.

Contents

Chapter 1: Inside the Spaghetti Bowl 1

Chapter 2: Coming to America 15

Chapter 3: Pride in Your Work 25

Chapter 4: Vote—It Is Your Duty 31

Chapter 5: 'The Una Storia Segreta,' 'The Secret Story.' 37

Chapter 6: Message to Grandchildren 47

Chapter 7: Superman Can't Die 65

Chapter 8: Italian Grandparents, Holidays, Traditions, and Curses 73

Chapter 9: A Real Love Story 93

Chapter 10: You Will Graduate from College if It Kills Us Both 99

Chapter 11: The Beginning of the End 105

Chapter 12: Life with Integrity 115

Chapter 13: Reunion at Heaven's Gate 137

Chapter 14: Are All These People Related to Us? 143

Chapter 15: The Italian Stigma 153

Chapter 16: Yes, All These People Are Related to Us 161

Chapter 17: The Eulogy 167

Chapter 18: The Final Resting Place 173

Chapter 19: A Grandmother's Memories 177

Chapter 1:

Inside the Spaghetti Bowl

The squeaky clean smell of antiseptic starched the air. The sounds of people speaking in urgent but hushed tones could be heard in the overcrowded room where my mother, Carmela (Carm Zaccari), lay in her hospital bed surrounded by my father, three brothers, two sisters, all of my nieces and nephews, and my Aunt Mary (Mom's sister). My brother Frank nudged his teenage daughter Sara and quietly said, "Look around the room. Whom do you see?"

"Family."

Frank replied, "That's right, because when it really matters, all that you have is your family. Look at Grandpa. They have been married for fifty-seven years, and he is still there holding her hand. That's what family and unconditional love is all about. As you get older and start thinking about marriage, I want you to remember this scene. I want you to make sure that you are positive that the man you marry will be there holding your hand fifty-seven years later at your death bed.

My sister Annette, standing next to Frank, said, "That is right. With Italian families, when one of us is tickled, we all laugh. When one of us is cut, we all bleed." Sara's eyes started to tear up. Frank asked Sara if she was OK. "If this is scaring you, we can leave."

She said no, she wasn't scared and felt it was her place to be here with Grandma. "If it were me that was sick, Grandma wouldn't leave, so I am not leaving her." Sara put her head down to try to hide her tears.

Aunt Mary was sitting quietly in a corner of the room next to Sara. She leaned toward Sara and told her, "I remember when they first met." She smiled at the memory and told Sara the story: "It was 1950. I had just become engaged to Sam Crea. We had a party to announce the engagement. It was the first time these two large Italian families would meet. Your grandma and I are standing next to each other. Carm whispers to me, 'Who is that guy in the brown suit?'

"I glanced over and said, 'That's Frank Zaccari; he is Sam's cousin. He is going to be one of Sam's ushers for the wedding.'

"Carm whispered, 'I hope he doesn't wear that ugly suit. Brown is definitely not his color.' We both laughed. You know how infectious your grandmother's laugh is, right? So I tell her, 'Shhh, stop it Carm. He is coming this way.'

"Your grandpa walks up to Carm and says, 'Hi, I am Frank Zaccari; you must be one of Mary's older sisters.' Carm turned, and with a look that could melt the polar ice caps, said, 'I'm Carm, Mary's *younger* sister, thank you very much.'

"Well, your grandpa didn't believe her, and he says, 'No kidding; How old are you?'

"Carm gives him another glare. 'I'm seventeen. Just what are you trying to imply?'

'You're lying,' your grandpa said with a sneer.

"Carm turned to me and said, 'Mary, tell Mr. Tact here how old I am.'" Aunt Mary touched Sara on the shoulder and said, 'It was love at first sight.'"

At this point everyone in the room was listening to the story. Sara forced a smile and said, "Really? Grandpa, you really said *that*?"

My sister Mary Anne leaned over and said out of the corner of her mouth, "Aunt Mary, that's not how I heard the story."

Aunt Mary gave her a sideways glance and the backhanded wave that every Italian learns at birth, and says in a mock Italian accent, "Non jou tell my secrets."

Mom, laughing, then said to Sara, "Your grandfather was a real smooth talker, huh. How could I resist that opening line?" The whole room exploded with laughter.

"Grandpa, how did you propose to Grandma?" Sara asked.

"He handed me a ring and said, '*Here*,'" Mom said with a smirk.

Dad argued back, "I did not! I took her out for a nice dinner and then I asked her if she would like to have dinner with me for the next fifty or sixty years. *Then* I handed her the ring."

Sara looked warmly at her grandparents and says wistfully, "Aww…that is so sweet."

"Sweet!" Her grandfather said with just the slightest hint of mock irritation. "It was the most expensive dinner I ever had."

Mom squeezed Dad's hand and answered, "It was worth every penny, but he just won't admit it." They gave each other a smile and nod that let everyone know it was more than worth every penny. It was the start of fifty-seven years of love and devotion. In that moment, the years seemed to vanish from their faces, and they looked as happy as they were the moment Mom accepted the ring.

After another hour of visiting, stories, and a great deal of laughter, Mom said to my brother Tony, "Go take your brother Steve back to the hotel, and help him get ready for bed." Steve is a quadriplegic from a car accident twenty-four years earlier. He has to be on strict diet and sleeping program, or he could get very sick. For example, he has to be turned from side to side every three hours while he is sleeping, or he could get bed sores. Tony got Steve in bed around midnight and left Steve with our nephew Chris. Tony and his wife, Penny, returned to the hospital to be with Mom and the rest of my family.

When they got back to the hospital, Mom was sleeping. She woke up around 1:30 a.m. She was very weak and asked in a whispered tone, "I'm still alive? What time is it?" After we told her, "Yes, you are still alive," and what time it was, she said, "Well, my father died at three o'clock in the morning; maybe I will, too."

Tony told her, "No, Mom, three o'clock is not good for me; I have to go back to the hotel and turn Steve. Can we pick another time? Maybe we can do lunch. Have your people call my people."

My mother smiled. "Smart ass."

Tony said, "No, Mom, I'm shit head; Frank is smart ass." My mother smiled and drifted back to sleep.

At 2:45 a.m., she woke up again and said, "Hey, go to your brother." She was the ultimate mother right to the end. Tony told her, "Don't go anywhere, and I will bring Steve back here in the morning." She promised, and Tony left. He brought Steve back to the hospital around 9:00 a.m., and we all had a chance to say our last goodbyes.

All this occurred Sunday, September 20, 2009. Mom was awake and alert. It was as if she was patiently waiting for her children and grandchildren to arrive so she could have her last moments with each. Somehow we knew she would not allow herself to die until she had time to have a private last word with each of her children and grandchildren.

When my family arrived, Mom was in the hospital bed connected to a morphine IV and oxygen. The doctor explained that over the next couple days, Mom would become weaker and may experience more pain. The morphine was to make sure she was as comfortable as possible. As she became weaker, the morphine would be increased. This would put her into a coma, and her organs would start to shut down. It should be over within three to four days.

Mom knew the end was near. She had been planning this for the last few years. Two years ago we learned that Mom had a heart valve that was failing. If she didn't have surgery, the valve would eventually stop working and she would die. The doctors recommended open-heart surgery, but Mom refused. Mary Anne asked, "How long are we talking about without the surgery?" The answer was,

"It could be a week, a month, a year, or five years. We don't know, but it will not improve without the surgery."

Mom said, "I already had two major cancer surgeries. I am a two-time cancer survivor. I have had both knees and one hip replaced. I am diabetic and not in the best of health. Even if I survive the surgery and the rehab, how long will this extend my life—maybe two years, and my quality of life will be terrible. I am not going through this at this point in my life. I have lived long enough, and I am ready for whatever happens." We all felt fortunate that we had the last two years.

For the past two years, Mom had been giving away things to her children and grandchildren. She was putting together lists of where everything was and what needed to be done. She had prepared packets for each of her five children, eight grandchildren, and one great-grandchild. The clothes she wanted to wear, the style of her hair, what she wanted in the coffin with her, what readings she wanted at her funeral, who the pall bearers were to be, and even which of the family cemetery plots she wanted as her final resting place. As always, she had addressed every detail. She did not want her family to be burdened with her death and funeral.

We watched Mom's health continue to deteriorate. We saw it at her grandson Chris's wedding in July. We saw it again in August when everyone came home as Mom started hospice care. We knew the end was near. While we knew the call was coming, it didn't make it any easier when on Saturday, September 19, 2009, Mary Anne made the call to my brothers, Frank, Anthony, (Tony), Steve, and sister Annette, saying that Mom was in the hospital under hospice care and requested that all treatment stop. As a hospice patient, any number of people can visit at any time, day or night. Sadly we all knew this was going to be the end.

We packed up our families and started the journey back to Dunkirk, New York, from Sacramento, Phoenix, Rochester, and Buffalo. During the next eight days, the Zaccari family went through every emotion imaginable. Hundreds of family and friends came to the hospital to see and talk to Mom one final time. As loved ones came to visit, both the hospital room and our parents' house were filled with laughter, tears, food, and stories. We learned so much about our family. We heard stories about their journey to America, their struggle to live the American dream, the joys of weddings and births, and the heartaches of death and illness. The stories filled us with pride and joy.

My cousin Sandra said, "The story of this family needs to be written. People need to know what it was like to grow up Italian in the '60s and '70s; or in your case, Frank, the '50s."

Mary Anne added, "It would make a great book. People could relate to the way things used to be when families lived close together and helped each other and got together frequently to celebrate life."

Tony said, "Most of the country thinks that growing up Italian is like those morons on the television show *Jersey Shore*." Frank asked, "What is this *Jersey Shore* thing?"

Another cousin answered, "You know the reality show where the women all shop off the wrong racks, and a guy walks around holding up his shirt? They all live in one house and are drunk and get in fights all the time."

"Happy to say I have never seen the show. Not the image of growing up Italian that I remember," Frank replied.

Now don't get us wrong—we have nothing against the people on *Jersey Shore*. They caught lightening in a bottle and made a bunch of money, which we hope they save. But with all that Italians have contributed to this country, it's sad that the two images that most people relate "Italians" with are *Jersey Shore* and organized crime.

My brother Frank said, "Do you know how long that would take to compile all these stories and write a book?"

My brother Anthony said, "And besides, who would read it?" "I would read it," A little voice said from behind them. They turned around to see Leah, Annette's five-year-old daughter whom she adopted from China. Leah was holding Tony's fourteen-month-old grandson Ethan.

"I could read it to Ethan, after I learn how to read chapter books."

Then I whispered into Frank's ear, "Here is your opening sentence. Write this down." He looked around the room and found a piece of paper. My brother Tony handed him a pen. He wrote, "The squeaky clean smell of antiseptec starched the air."

My brother Steve glanced at the paper and said, "You spelled *antiseptic* wrong. You two buttheads are going to need my help." You see, my three brothers actually put pen to paper, but I gave them the words; well, Mom and I gave them the words. They literally wrote some of this book in their sleep.

For example, one night Tony had a dream. I told him, "Write it down." When he woke up the next morning, he had forgotten the dream. It wasn't until a few days later when he found a piece of paper on his nightstand with these words written in his own handwriting, "It was the single most gut-wrenching, heart-breaking thing that we ever had the privilege of doing. We stood there looking at the first face our eyes ever recognized, we held the hand that first touched us so lovingly; and we were grateful to be there so that we could be the last face she would see, the last touch that she would feel." They were thinking about writing a eulogy, but how do you sum up a life of seventy-seven years into seven minutes: her aspirations, her reservations, her pains, her joys, her successes, her disappointments, her sorrows, her love.

"That's your story," I told him, but I am getting a little ahead of myself.

So, my brothers, Tony, the family historian; Frank, the writer; and Steve, the editor, started to talk about writing this book. They started to collect stories about the family and what we all remembered about growing up Italian. They struggled over what to name the book. Naming it *Growing Up Italian* didn't capture the complexity of a family. There are so many components that make up a family that is just starting its fourth generation in America. What title could symbolize all these components? How do we combine the original family members, marriages, divorces, births, deaths, traditions, culture, good times, and bad times? Frank mentioned this to one of his customers, a seventy-year-old man named Charles Walker. Mr. Walker is a former Marine and Korean War Veteran.

While he is not Italian, he understood what Frank was saying. He suggested *Inside the Spaghetti Bowl*, saying "With spaghetti, everything is mixed in together: the pasta, the sauce, meatballs, sausage, cheese, and all the spices. You throw everything in together, and miraculously it all works. Sometimes it comes out great, sometimes not so much, just like a family." He was right. What is in this spaghetti bowl that makes up the Zaccari/Mancuso family? The ingredients are as follows:

- Stories of passion and humor blended in perfect harmony and served up with love and a sprinkling of faith.

- Stories of proud men and courageous women.

- Stories of veracity and respect shining like a midnight star.

- Stories of undying love and heartbreaking gallantry.

- Stories of integrity carved in stone.

- Stories of family honor and unfaltering loyalty.

- Stories of tragedy and setbacks colliding with winning determination.

- Stories of valor set in gold.

- Stories of how to live and die with grace and dignity.

It is our story; it is your story. It is a story for every beating heart that has loved or has been loved. It is the story about the struggles and pains endured by those virtuous individuals who poured their lives into ours and filled our years with intimate memories and a gladdened heart. It is the story you will want to pass down to your children and grandchildren.

This book is not about the history of Italians in America, or what is was like to grow up Italian, and it certainly is not about how to make spaghetti. It is a book about family and unconditional love through the good times and the bad. It is about a family who is and always will be there for each other no matter what. We hope that you see your family in this book, and that the memories make you smile.

Chapter 2:

Coming to America

On Sunday, September 20, my brother Frank, his two daughters, Stephanie and Sara, and my brother Steve all took a flight from Phoenix to Buffalo. On the way, Frank and Steve began the sad but needed task of writing a eulogy. While they hoped it would not be necessary, they both knew it would.

When the plane landed, they picked up the handicap-accessible van and started the drive to our hometown of Dunkirk, New York. The main attraction in town was Lake Erie, but the city never did anything to build up the waterfront. Dunkirk was once a steel town, but over the past forty-plus years, the city had deteriorated like so many steel towns. Billy Joel's song "Allentown" could have been written about Dunkirk:

> Well we're living here in Allentown
> And they're closing all the factories down
> Out in Bethlehem they're killing time

Filling out forms
Standing in line.

It was sad what happened to this community, but to our parents, Frank and Carm Zaccari, it was home. They spent their entire life in the Dunkirk area. My siblings, Frank, Mary Anne, Anthony (Tony), Annette, and Steve all left as soon as they could. All tried unsuccessfully for over forty years to get our parents to move. Mom and Dad would have none of it. This is where their parents had settled when they left Italy and Sicily in the early 1900s. This is where they were raised, where their children were raised, where their family and friends lived and were buried. They had opportunities to move to Delaware to work for DuPont and to California to work in the aerospace industry, but this was their home.

The old neighborhood was a shadow of its former self. It was run down and uncared for except for our parents' house and our neighbor directly across the street. As the van pulled up to the house, fifteen-year-old Sara said, "Oh my god, this looks like the neighborhood in the movie *Grand Torino.*"

She was right. The exterior of the neighborhood was sad and depressing, but when you walked into my parents' home, you could feel the love, you could smell the wonderful aroma of Italian food, you could enjoy conversations with friends and family. When you were in their home, you knew you were loved and accepted without conditions. Everyone who entered that house became family. We had a saying: "The first time you are here, you will be served, so that you know where everything is kept in the kitchen. The second time, help yourself to whatever you want and clean up after yourself. The third time, hey, as long as you are up, make me a sandwich, too."

After the bags were dropped off at the house, everyone headed to the hospital. Mom was awake and alert, surrounded by Dad, her children, grandchildren, several nieces, and her sister Aunt Mary. She had been waiting for her granddaughters to arrive from California. Mom asked the girls, "How was the flight?" They both answered, "Long." Mom and Aunt Mary both laughed.

Aunt Mary said, "Your Great-Grandmother Mancuso use to say in broken English, 'Why do you complain. People can fly across the country in six hours. They give you food and drink. When I came from Sicily, it took thirty days on a boat.'"

Aunt Mary added, "'And they didn't have a stateroom on the boat either. It was worse than the steerage section from the movie *Titanic*.'"

Like the vast majority of Italians and Sicilians who came to the United States the early 1900s, our family came for the hope of a better life. In Italy and Sicily, what you were is what you and your family would be forever. There was little hope to improve one's lot in life. America, however, was the Promised Land. It was the land of opportunity. It was the land where the streets were paved with gold. America offered hope. Hope for advancement. Hope for the future.

Hope for a chance. So as teenagers, they left all their family, friends, worldly belongings, and the only life they had ever known with simply the hope—not a promise or guarantee—just the hope of a better life.

They booked passage on less than sanitary and often overcrowded boats, and I use the term *boat* very loosely. They spent thirty or more days at sea battling hunger and sickness. If they were lucky, they suffered only from seasickness the entire time. I often heard family members who made that trip say "When we saw the Statue of Liberty, everyone cheered and celebrated. We were all so happy. We knew that while maybe *our* lives would not be easier, our children and grandchildren would have a better life." Talk about courage and unconditional love.

Our maternal grandfather Francesco Mancuso arrived first on July 10, 1900. He listed his occupation as a "grinder" and forever renounced all allegiance and fidelity to any foreign prince, potentate, state, or sovereignty, and particularly to Victor Emmanuel III, King of Italy. Nearly twenty years later on March 8, 1920, our grandfather Antonio Zaccari, a blacksmith, arrived. What both discovered is that the streets were not paved with gold. In fact most of the streets in Brooklyn were not paved at all. The United States is the single greatest country in the world, but it is not a kind place to the latest group of immigrants, particularly any group who speaks a different language and has dark skin. Many Italians, particularly the lighter-skinned Northern Italians, often dropped the vowel at the end of their name in order to sound more American. Nonetheless, they were in America and were both eager and excited to live the "American dream."

Our maternal grandmother came to America under completely different circumstances. Her parents, Biaggo and Lucia Battaglia, were planning to move to America in the late 1800s. What pleased them the most was that Lucia was pregnant, and their new baby (our grandmother) would be born in America. As they were making the final arrangements for their trip to America, a jealous neighbor shot and killed Biaggo as he was walking home from his last day of work. Lucia gave birth to our grandmother on January 1, 1892, and named her Biagga after her father. Lucia never gave up on her quest go to America. When her son Carmelo and daughter Ineifia were turning twenty, she sent them to America with the hope that she and Biagga would join them when she could save up enough money. But times were difficult in Sicily for a widow, so Lucia had to remarry. She never achieved her dream of living in America.

In America, Ineifia met our grandfather Frank Mancuso. They married in 1903. They settled in Couderport, Pennsylvania, where Ineifia had her first child, a son that they named Giuseppe. In 1906 Ineifia died in childbirth. The baby lived and our grandfather named her Ineifia, after her mother, but he would always call her Fifi. (She would later be known as Grace.) Grandpa wrote to his mother-in-law, Lucia, to tell her that Ineifia had died and that he now had two children without a mother. He asked for permission to marry her other daughter Biagga who was only fourteen years old. Lucia agreed to this because it meant that Biagga could live in America. Biagga plead with her Mother not to send her away, but Lucia would say, "Who would better care for these children than the sister of their mother."

So my grandfather returned to Sicily and brought Biagga to America. He had originally left Sicily just before he turned twenty years old and before he served his two-year mandatory service in the Army. The government was waiting for him to return to Italian soil so that they could put him into the military. A government agent questioned Lucia before Frank arrived in Sicily. When my grandfather came to Sicily, Lucia warned him that he had to leave immediately, so he left with Biagga before they were married. They left in the middle of the night, down the mountain on a donkey, to the dock where their ship would take them to America. All they had was sixty dollars. Accompanying them on their journey to America was Antonio and Nina Albanese (brother and sister to Lucia). The voyage on the ship was long and difficult for Biagga. My grandmother said that she threw up every day during the thirty-day trip. When they arrived in Couderport, Pennsylvania, in a horse and buggy, Biagga asked, "Why did you bring me here to this wilderness?" But when she saw her precious niece and nephew Fifi and Giuseppe for the first time, she knew why she was brought across the ocean to this home. Frank and Biagga were married at St. Eulalia Church on August 5,

1907, five days after they arrived on Ellis Island. From then on, our grandmother raised her sister's two children as if they were her own. Exactly nine months to the day of their wedding, Biagga (now known as Bessie) gave birth to her first child on May 5, 1908. They named him Biaggo after his grandfather who was shot and killed as he was making preparations to move to America. (This child would later be known as Russell.)

Can you imagine, at the age of fifteen, leaving your mother to go marry a man that you never met, is twice your age, and having to raise his two children in a country where you could not speak the language? To this day it amazes me what our grandmother experienced, not to mention that she had ten more children and would outlive four. However, one of the saddest times for Grandma, the story that would always make her cry when she told us, was about her mother. The plan was always that some day her mother, Lucia, would join her in America. When she had saved up enough money to bring her mother to America, she wrote her (actually she dictated the letter to one of her children, since grandma could not read or write) with great pride and asked her mother to come to America. Her mother replied back that she would not come to America. Her reasons were that she was old and feared that her grandchildren would not treat her with respect.

Grandma's response was, "If you will not come here, then you can forget that you have a family in America!"

Lucia replied, "My dear daughter, I will never forget that my blood is in America."

This touched our grandmother so much that she immediately had a letter written back and apologized, but sadly, Lucia died before the letter arrived. She would later tell us, "There are two things when lost that can never be restored, your soul and your mother."

After a visit to Ellis Island in July 2007, Tony wrote this letter to his infant grandson and to the next generations of the Zaccari/Mancuso bloodline.

Dear Ethan and any of your brothers or sisters or cousins,

My Grandmother Bessie (Battaglia) Mancuso was born on January 1, 1892. Take care of yourself, eat healthy, and exercise your body and mind so that on January 1, 2092, you could sit with your grandchildren and tell them these stories that are written here for you. They will probably roll their eyes and not be interested, but tell them anyway. It is important that they know what their great-great-great-grandmother did so many years ago.

In July of 2007, your Grandmother Penny, your Aunt Cherish, and I went on vacation. We stayed at a hotel in the Meadowlands of New Jersey. We got up one morning and caught an early morning bus to New York City. We got off at the Port Authority Bus Terminal. From there we got a tour bus that took us around the City. It was a hot day, 90 degrees plus, but we enjoyed a two-hour sightseeing tour. We got off at Battery Park and stood in line to get on the Ferry that would take us to the Statue of Liberty and Ellis Island. By the time we got to Ellis Island, we were hungry so your Grandmother and I went to order some food. When we got to the front of the line, a very nice young lady waited on us. She said that we looked exhausted. We were exhausted. I am telling you this story so that you could compare it to July of 1907 when my Grandmother Bessie (Battaglia) Mancuso came to Ellis Island as a fifteen-year-old girl. She left her country, her home, and her mother, and she would never see them again. She traveled for thirty days by boat. She told us that she suffered seasickness every day. She said that she cried every day because she missed her mother. Your Grandmother and I were exhausted after traveling several hours, and three days later we would be back home in our own beds. My Grandmother traveled for thirty days to get to that same spot and never went home again. Tell your grandchildren the tremendous sacrifice made so that we could live in this great country and never take that for granted.

After a very short stay in the Pennsylvania and Brooklyn areas, both grandfathers independently moved to a community outside of Buffalo, New York. To paraphrase a routine by the late great comedian Richard Jeni, "So the family moved to Buffalo which begs the question why? Let's see now we are accustomed to the crime and the poverty in Brooklyn, but it just isn't cold enough. I know let's move to Buffalo." So in the communities of Fredonia and Dunkirk, cities less than three miles apart, Frank Mancuso and Anthony Zaccari started their families.

In 1921 and 1925 our grandfathers and grandmothers became United States citizens. On the day they became citizens, they stood a little straighter, held their heads a little higher, and stuck out their chests a little further. They let their children and their grandchildren know every day that it is both an honor and a privilege to be an American citizen and it is our duty to work hard, vote, support our President, do whatever it takes to make this country better, and if necessary be prepared to protect and defend the United States.

Chapter 3:

Pride in Your Work

On Monday morning, September 21, Mom was still alert. Family and friends came and went all day long. Most of the visitors were friends and relatives about Mom's age and older. This was the old guard. Most were first-generation Americans. They were all retired now, but they had worked very hard their entire lives and took great pride in their work. At one point Uncle Marion, Mom's brother (who was a barber), Aunt Mary (who had worked at the local college), Uncle Sam (who had worked for a newspaper company), and our father (who had worked as a machinist) were all in the room. They all shared stories about the old days and all the jobs they performed to survive and to provide for their families. Mom said to all her grandchildren, "Listen to these stories. You come from a family that takes great pride in their work. Remember, whatever you do for a living, do it the best you can every day. This way people will say 'You know that Carm Zaccari, her grandchildren are all very successful and good-looking, too. You all look like me.'"

This brought more laughter, and then she added, "Always be thankful you are in America. Back in Italy people didn't have a choice of what they wanted to do."

Being an American was the ultimate dream for every Italian we knew or met growing up. The Italians brought so much to this country. Their contributions can be seen in every area, from the arts, music, food, culture, industry, fashion, architecture, sports, and entertainment. To hear our grandparents and parents talk, the best and most successful people in every field were Italian. So we would challenge them and say, "Oh yeah? Who is the greatest singer?" They have several - Mario Lanza, Pavarotti, Frank Sinatra, Tony Bennett, Frankie Valli, and the great Andrea Bocelli, whom Celine Dion once referred to as "The voice of God." It doesn't get any better than that. "What about the greatest actor?" They rattled off: Robert De Niro, Al Pacino, Sophia Loren, and John Travolta. "OK. What about sports?" we'd ask. They would quickly reply, "Joe DiMaggio, Yogi Berra, Joe Montana, and Tommy Lasorda." Whatever the field of endeavor, they had a number of names. But was most impressive to us was not the famous people; it was the everyday, working Italian-American. Many Italians helped build or worked on the railroads, city infrastructure, worked in steel, on assembly lines, farms, factories, and served in the military. It didn't matter what they did, they did it with great pride. We heard every day growing up, "It doesn't matter what you choose to do, but whatever it is, do the best you can every day." It was usually followed by this story: Three men were working on a construction site. Someone asked the first man, "What are you doing?"

He grunted and said, "I'm working."

They asked the second man and he said, "I am laying bricks."

But when they asked the third man, who was an Italian, he said with great pride, "I am building a great new Cathedral where people will come and thank God they are Americans."

Grandma Zaccari's father was Filippo Saglimben. He died in 1924 of cancer. After his death, the family did not have a penny in the house. Not only did they lose his income, but there were sizable bills from his illness. Even though Grandma and her sister Frances were working as sale clerks at the Boston Store in Dunkirk, they still were not earning enough money. Cousins and family friends were giving the family money and food, but they were still struggling.

A cousin took Grandma's brother Carl to the Dunkirk Radiator plant where Filippo used to work to ask the plant foreman for a job. Uncle Carl was only fifteen years old at the time. The plant foreman told them that he did not have a job for Carl. Seeing that the family was in desperate need of money, the plant foreman reached into his wallet and handed Carl a ten-dollar bill, which was a generous amount of money at that time.

Young Uncle Carl said, "No, thank you, sir. I don't want your money because next week my family and I are going to be in the same shape. I want to work. I want a job." Then he started to cry.

The following Monday young Carl had a job at the radiator plant sweeping floors. Once again I hear the words of our parents and grandparents: "It doesn't matter what you choose to do, but whatever it is, do it the best you can every day."

Tony tells a good story about pride in your work. When you grow up in a small town, it is common for many people to know your parents and grandparents. If you are Italian, you are probably related to many of those people. It was 1972. Tony was attending Cardinal Mindszenty High School. The story goes like this, "My father's first cousin Joe Damiano taught history and the big debate in the country and the school was whether or not to continue with the Apollo Program, the NASA program to land on the moon. The argument to discontinue space exploration was that diverting the money that was being spent to explore outer space could create many more jobs. Mr. D said, 'The space program was creating jobs.' Someone in the class argued, 'Only if you are an astronaut or rocket scientist.' Mr. D said, 'What if I told you that the father of someone in this class is employed by the space program?' Everyone demanded to know who, so Mr. D said, 'Tony, what does your father do for a living?' Tony said, 'My Dad is a machinist who builds the rocket booster of the Apollo rockets.' Then Mr. D added, 'And since Tony's Dad is paying tuition for five children that have attended or are attending this school, then you could say that I am, and this school is, indirectly benefiting from the space program.'

"I have always been proud of the work my father did, but that day I became a celebrity. Kids wanted to shake my hand; the smart kids, who I had little in common with, wanted to know if I had seen the rockets and what else had my father help build. I told them: the Gemini space capsule that put the first man into space and the Polaris missile used by the Navy. If you ask my Dad what he built that gave him the greatest satisfaction, he would always say, 'The rescue capsule for nuclear submarines because it had the potential to save the life of someone who was risking his own life to protect and defend our country.' A health condition prevented my father from serving in active duty in World War II, but he still found a way to serve the country with his job." Like the words to the Montgomery Gentry song, *That's something to be proud of*!

Later in the morning, a well-dressed man in his late forties came into Mom's room. She recognized him immediately and smiled brightly, "Rock! It's so nice to see you." She threw her arms up to hug Rock, and then said, "Rock, I would like you to meet my son Frank. Frank, Rock is the principal of our high school."

"Vice Principal," Rock politely corrects her as he shakes hands with Frank. "Hello, nice to meet you."

"Vice Principal only until they realize how good you are. And this is Frank's daughter Sara."

"It's nice to meet you, Sara." Rock told her, "Your grandmother taught me so much when I was a new teacher at Holy Trinity School." Sara smiled politely, not quite sure what to say. She had never been on a first-name basis with a vice principal.

"So Rock," Mom asked, "How have you been?"

Frank motions to Sara for them to step back and give them a moment to talk. When they were far enough away, Sara whispered to her father, "I thought grandma was just a secretary."

"That is a perfect example of what I have been telling you." Frank saw an opportunity for a life lesson. "It doesn't matter what you choose to do for a living, but whatever it is, do it the best you can every day. Grandma was, as you put it, 'just a secretary,' but she put her heart and soul into her job. She had an impact on Rock when he was just a young teacher. She encouraged him and believed in him when he didn't even believe in himself. Grandma gave him the confidence to not give up. Because Grandma inspired him by her passion for education, just think about how many other young lives he has influenced as a teacher and now as a vice principal. It is so important to do your best every day because you never know what you do or say that will touch so many others, and you may never know how far your influence will reach."

The usually stoic Sara smiled with pride as she thought about her grandmother's legacy.

Chapter 4:

Vote—It Is Your Duty

Early Monday afternoon many of the third-generation Zaccari/Mancuso cousins arrived at the hospital. Our cousin Kathy, who is a Catholic Eucharistic minister (this means she has been authorized by the Catholic Church to bring communion to people, which is a very high honor in the Church), came by with her daughters Kristin and Megan. While Kathy administered communion to Mom, her daughters got reacquainted with Frank's daughters, Stephanie and Sara. Kristin, who had just started her senior year in high school, announced that she officially became an adult by turning eighteen. After some congratulations from everyone in the room, Frank asked her, "Have you registered to vote yet?" Kristin looked at him like he was crazy.

Mary Anne added, "Well, have you? You've been eighteen for three days already."

Kristin said, "You people are all crazy!" This led her grandmother (Aunt Mary) to announce that voting is taken very serious in this family.

Voting in *every* election, no matter how trivial the position, was treated with a solemn respect. Our grandparents and parents never missed an election. They would pay attention to the candidates and the issues, and many discussions occurred after dinners. If someone had the audacity to say, "Who cares which person gets elected?" and they were far enough away not to get slapped in the head, they would hear this story: "I came to America so you could have opportunities that we never had in the old country." (Did you ever notice that our grandparents never referred to Italy or Sicily by name. It was always "the old country.") "In the old country, we had no ability to choose our leaders. There was a king, and whoever was next in line to the throne became king. It didn't matter if they were as dumb as a rock; they became king. Here in America, we, the people, choose. Voting is your single greatest right as an American citizen. If I have to drag you by the hair to the polling place, you will vote in every election." While none of the family actually believed they would have dragged anyone by the hair, no one wanted to find out, so every election meant that every Zaccari and Mancuso who was of age was at the polls.

Every Italian we knew who was my parents' age or older had survived the Great Depression. They took nothing for granted and could pinch a penny until Lincoln had a blood blister. As Depression survivors, President Roosevelt was their hero. In their minds, he saved the country and made it possible for them to continue to have a life in America. Largely because of President Roosevelt, every Italian we ever met growing up was a Democrat.

My family voted a straight Democratic ticket every election, except one. At that time, the Italians were not held in high regard. As the most recent immigrants, we lived in the worst area of town, had trouble getting a job, or even finding a place to live. There was no fair housing or employment laws back then. Due to the phenomenon I later learned was called "de facto segregation," we all lived in the same few blocks. The story of that one exception, as it was told to us, was that an Italian man was running for mayor of Dunkirk. He was a light-skinned Northern Italian who had dropped the vowel from his last name and was doing all he could to disassociate himself from the Italian community. Rumor had it he made the statement he did not want or need the Italian vote.

His opponent, a non-Italian Republican came to the Columbus Club, the local Italian social club, to see Grandpa Zaccari. Grandpa Z was President of the Columbus Club and could read and write English, so he was a man the neighborhood trusted and respected. Over a meal and some wine, the candidate told our grandfather the comments made by the Italian candidate. Grandpa listened, and then said, "You know, many of my family and friends were trained in construction and carpentry in the old country. I see all the building and construction going on in this community, but I don't see any Italians doing the work. If you want my help, then you need to see that some of these people get jobs with the city."

The candidate said, "Of course, Mr. Zaccari, you will be the first one to get a job."

"I have a job. I am talking about these younger men with young children to raise and feed."

The candidate said he would see to it that Italians were considered and hired. With that my grandfather instructed the candidate to arrange for transportation to drive the people to and from the polls. On Election Day, my grandfather walked to the polls, voted, then drew a picture of the inside of the election booth, highlighting the lever that would place a vote for the Republican candidate. He walked back to the Columbus Club and made several copies of the drawing. He then spoke to all the club members and their spouses, handed them the drawing and strongly suggested why they should vote for the Republican candidate. The Republican won a very close election and Italians were finally hired by the city. My grandfather asked nothing for himself. Now, we don't know how much this story has been embellished over the years, but one fact in indisputable. Our grandfather was a good and honest man who lived his life with integrity. In fact, the motto on the Zaccari Family crest reads, *Life with Integrity*.

Vote—It Is Your Duty

For Grandma Mancuso, voting was on par with going to church. Since she didn't drive, she would get up, put on her Sunday best, and walk more than two miles to her polling place. Of course, most elections were in November, so the story was that her walk "was uphill in the snow, both ways." Grandma could not read or write English. Her signature was an "X." This was very common back in the day. On one particular Election Day, Grandma walked to the polling location, but the poll worker refused to let her vote. The worker didn't understand her broken English, and since she couldn't point out her name on the voter roll, the worker refused to let her vote. Grandma was outraged. She said in her broken English, "I am an American citizen. How dare you refuse my right to vote!"

The worker told her to leave. She left, but she didn't go home. She walked three miles to city hall and right into the mayor's office. The mayor, a man named Russell Joy, whose family also emigrated from Italy (although they had dropped the vowel), listened to her story and became more outraged than Grandma. The mayor called the police chief and had the chief drive her and the mayor back to the polling location. The mayor read the poll workers the riot act and threatened them with whatever crime he could. As the story goes, his tirade ended with, "How dare you refuse an American citizen, who left her country as a teenager and endured great hardship to come to America, the right to vote. If I could throw you in jail right now, I would." When the mayor finished, Grandma said something to the poll worker in Italian that inferred the workers parents were just casual friends, walked into the election booth, and voted. Mayor Joy waited for her to finish, then instructed the police chief to drive her to the store so she could buy her groceries, and then drive her home. The next time you don't feel like voting, think about this story.

Chapter 5:

'The Una Storia Segreta,' 'The Secret Story.'

Later Monday evening, Aunt Mary's oldest daughter, Sandra, stopped by the hospital. The Crea's and the Zaccari's were as close as two families could possibly be. We lived within two blocks of each other. We had five children and Aunt Mary had six. The children were all about the same age. We all played together and went to school and church together. In fact many people weren't sure which child belonged to which family. Aunt Mary was the Zaccaris' "second mother," and Aunt Carm was the Creas'.

While we were all preparing to lose a wife, mother, sister, aunt, and grandmother, Sandra had suffered a parent's greatest nightmare. Her daughter Sara Pieszak had died two years earlier after a long and courageous battle with leukemia. Sara Pieszak was just twenty years old. Sara was always happy and smiling. She made everyone around her feel good. She was an organizer who encouraged her family and friends to get involved. If her sister or brother or cousins were hesitant or apprehensive about doing something, Sara would take them by the hand and walk them through the process. While we could still see the hurt and sorrow in Sandra's eyes, we also knew she was at peace knowing that her child was the family's ambassador in heaven.

When Sandra arrived, Mom asked if there was any news about the adoption process that Tom and his wife, Martha, were navigating (Tom is Aunt Mary's youngest son). Tom was born less than one month before Steve. The two were inseparable all through high school. Tom went to the University of Dayton and joined ROTC. He had recently married and retired as an Army Colonel. Tom and Martha were enduring a long adoption process without success.

Frank's daughter Stephanie asked, "Is Tom the one that flew the Blackhawk helicopter?"

The entire room looked at Stephanie with shock. "How do you know about the Blackhawk helicopter?" someone asked.

"In high school my friends and I played a video game that used the Blackhawk. Plus he came to visit us in Seattle."

Mary Anne's son Nick said, "It seems like a lot of the family were in the military." He was right. Pete Crea, Tom's uncle, retired from the Air Force. Tom retired from the Army. Sam Crea served in World War II. Frank Crea, Tom's

'The Una Storia Segreta,' 'The Secret Story.'

brother, is an aeronautical engineer for the Navy. Dad was a machinist who worked on many military projects. My brother Frank served in the Air Force during the Vietnam War and Mom's brother Sam served in World War II.

"How come so many of our family were in the military?" Nick asked. The answer was simple. It is our duty as Americans.

World War II was a major milestone, both in American history and for the Italian community. Italy, under the reign of Benito Mussolini, had sided with Hitler. This meant that the United States, the country that every Italian we ever met had dreamed of and sacrificed so much to be a part of, would be at war with Italy. For some Italians, this was a dilemma. A few of the old Italians would say, "We come to America and now America is going to drop bombs on the homes of our parents." This was not the sentiment of the overwhelming number of Italian-Americans. It was certainly not even a point of discussion for our family. Every Zaccari and Mancuso family member who was of age enlisted in the military. All that was said is, "We are Americans. We left the old country for the opportunities that America provides and now America needs us." We were fortunate. All of our family members returned home from the war. Mom's brother Sam was wounded, but he made it back.

My brother Frank recalled watching a Public Television show called *The Italians,* which highlighted the contributions of Italian-Americans. The one area that caught his attention was the statement, "That while they were the last of the Europeans to migrate to America and that Italy under Mussolini had sided with Hitler, more Italian-Americans served and died for the United States than any other ethnic group." This didn't surprise us. Every Italian we know wants to be an American in every way, shape, and form. If our country needs us to protect and defend it, we will rise to the occasion. I am proud to say that a Zaccari/Mancuso has served in every armed conflict since World War II.

Those who did not serve in active duty found other ways to serve our country. For example, July 21, 1969, the day Neil Armstrong and Buzz Aldrin walked on the moon, our family, like everyone else in the world, was transfixed on the television. We were in total amazement as we watched the two ghostly white figures step off of the ladder onto the surface of the moon. Our cousin Frank Crea was about seventeen years old. He always had a great interest in aerospace and the space program. He watched with great intensity. Grandma Mancuso watched it with him. "Frankie," she said in her thick Italian accent, "non jou believe. They only makin' foolish to jou." What she meant was, "They are trying to fool you because this isn't really happening. How can someone walk on the moon?"

"No Grandma, this is happening right now. Neil Armstrong and Buzz Aldrin are walking on the moon."

"Buzz?" she questioned, "What is *buzz*?"

"That's his name, Grandma."

"Who names a kid *Buzz*?" was her response. No one could convince Grandma that men were walking on the moon. It is understandable considering she was born before the invention of the airplane and even before Henry Ford started making cars. She traveled by donkey, ship, and horse-and-buggy, and now we were telling her that rockets put men on the moon. This was just too much for her.

However, young Frank not only believed what he saw, but believed the aerospace industry could become better. Today Frank Crea is an aeronautical engineer working for the United States Navy. Among his jobs are to design and test the aircraft that will defend and protect the United States. Given the air superiority of the U.S. military, I'd say he is doing a damn good job.

One of the downsides of wholeheartedly wanting to be an American is that many of our grandparents stopped speaking Italian around the grandchildren. We must have heard this line a thousand times, "We are Americans. Speak English." The older people would speak Italian to each other, but not to or around the grandchildren. Part of it was the pride of being an American, but part of it was fear that their grandchildren would speak with an accent and be subject to the discrimination and ridicule they endured.

While we understand their reasons, we are sorry we lost that part of our culture.

Somewhere around 1988 my brother Frank held the title of Government Operations Director for a high-tech company. He learned something about the Italians during World War II that shocked him. As he tells the story, "I had a meeting with Willie Brown, who was then the Speaker of the California State Assembly. During our meeting, Speaker Brown asked if I was Italian. I said 'Yes.' He then asked me if I was coming to the exhibit regarding the Italian Internment during World War II. He called it 'The Una Storia Segreta,' 'The Secret Story.'

"Speaker Brown noticed the shocked look on my face as he said, 'So I see you didn't know about this. It's true. It happened right here in San Francisco. Italians were interned at Treasure Island.'

"When I could finally speak I said, 'I never heard of this. I heard of the Japanese internment but never about the Italians.'

"Speaker Brown told me, 'The Italians never speak of it. It was a source of great embarrassment and shame for the Italian people that were affected. The government has not even acknowledged it. You come and see me next week when the exhibit is here at the Capitol.' I left the Speaker's office in shock. I called my parents to see if they had ever heard of the Italian Internment. They said they hadn't. I thought maybe it was just something on the West Coast.

I asked several families whose roots were in California, but again no one had heard of it, or at least no one was willing to talk."

"I went to the exhibit with a member of Speaker Brown's staff. I am still in shock. I recently purchased the book *Una Storia Segreta: The Secret History of Italian American Evacuation and Internment during World War II*. The book is edited with an Introduction by Lawrence DiStasi and published by Heyday Books of Berkeley, California. The back cover of the book and an essay that starts on page 10 by Rose D. Scherini, entitled 'When Italian Americans were Enemy Aliens' are very informative."

Frank also found United Senate Bill S. 1909.

SYNOPSIS:

A bill to provide for the preparation of a Governmental report detailing injustices suffered by Italian Americans during World War II, and a formal acknowledgement of such injustices by the President. **DATE OF INTRODUCTION:** November 10, 1999

SPONSOR(S): Sponsor and Cosponsors as of 11/18/1999, TORRICELLI, ROBERT G (D-NJ) — Sponsor

A subset of the Bill reads as follows:

The Congress makes the following findings:

(1) The freedom of more than 600,000 Italian-born immigrants in the United States and their families was

restricted during World War II by Government measures that branded them "enemy aliens" and included carrying identification cards, travel restrictions, and seizure of personal property.

(2) During World War II more than 10,000 Italian Americans living on the West Coast were forced to leave their homes and prohibited from entering coastal zones. More than 50,000 were subjected to curfews.

(3) During World War II thousands of Italian American immigrants were arrested, and hundreds were interned in military camps.

(4) Hundreds of thousands of Italian Americans performed exemplary service and thousands sacrificed their lives in defense of the United States.

(5) At the time, Italians were the largest foreign-born group in the United States, and today are the fifth largest immigrant group in the United States, numbering approximately 15,000,000.

(6) The impact of the wartime experience was devastating to Italian American communities in the United States, and its effects are still being felt.

(7) A deliberate policy kept these measures from the public during the war. Even 50 years later much information is still classified, the full story remains unknown

to the public, and it has never been acknowledged in any official capacity by the United States Government.

This actually happened, yet no one talks about it. To quote my Grandmother Mancuso when we would tell her about things that shocked or upset us - "What's done is done. Move on and forgive. Forgive but never forget and make sure this never happens again." The story must be told so that it does not happen again to another group of people. It is particularly important given the divisive polarization in this country between the left and the right. It's time for all our elected officials to be statesmen and stateswomen again and do the right thing for this country. It is time to stop the hatred and lack of cooperation and all the TV and radio commentators spewing hatred and divisiveness. We are one country. We can disagree without being disagreeable. Enough is enough!

Chapter 6:

Message to Grandchildren

Monday evening Annette and her husband, Dewey, arrived with their daughters Nicole and Leah. Leah is a precocious little five-year-old girl, adopted from China. Mom always referred to her as her "little China doll," which seemed to fit because she was tiny and had delicate, little features. She was, however, far from delicate and fragile. She was a tornado of energy, all arms and legs in constant motion. When she came into the hospital room that day, though, she was frozen with confusion and fear.

Mom gathered all her strength and said, "Leah, my little China doll. Come here and give me a hug." This seemed to unglue her feet from the floor and she rushed over to her grandma. Someone had to pick her up so that she could receive her hug as Mom beamed with pride and joy. Leah showed her grandmother her missing front tooth and explained in dramatic detail her tragic ordeal about losing it, as everyone listened in amusement.

Then Leah suddenly realized that her grandmother had not gotten out of bed yet, and she asked in heart-rending innocence, "Grandma, are you going to show me how to make pizza today? You said that you would when I get bigger."

Some of the sparkle left Mom's eyes as she said, "No, Honey…"

Tony interrupted before she could finish, "Leah, Grandma told me to teach you how to make pizza. As a matter of fact, I have been waiting for you to get here so that we could make pizza for dinner tonight." Tony turned toward Annette and said, "Why don't you stay here and visit with everyone. Penny, Dewey and I will take Leah back to Mom and Dad's house and start making dinner." Annette, who is a family counselor with a PhD, had been in social worker mode since she got off the plane. She had the task of coordinating Mom's care, her last wishes, and funeral arrangement. Annette needed some time with Mom to review the final details.

Since all her grandchildren were in the room, Mom said she wanted to talk to her grandchildren. All the adults but Aunt Mary, Annette, and Steve left. It was amazing to us how Mom had a special and unique relationship with each grandchild. This was particularly amazing, since four of them lived in New York, two in Phoenix, and two in California.

The first thing she said was, "I don't want any of you to be afraid or sad. Death is the final stage of life. I am not afraid. I am ready to go to heaven and see my parents, brothers and sisters, and my baby again. I will be waiting and getting a special place ready for all of you when you come to heaven many, many years from now. I want you all to know that my greatest joy in life was being married to your grandfather, raising our children, and being your grandmother. Each of you has brought me so much joy and happiness over the years. I have a package for each of you with many of the things you gave or sent to me over the years and some of my things I think you will like. I hope you keep this box, and whenever you think of me or miss me, open it and I will be there to listen and help you. My body won't be with you very much longer, but my spirit will be with you forever. I will be that little voice you hear in the back of your mind."

With that said, Mom told Annette to get the boxes for each grandchild. There were lots of smiles as her grandchildren looked at their individual boxes. They quickly put the boxes aside and all engaged in conversation together, sharing with each other and Mom what each was doing, their hopes, dreams, fears, and goals.

My nephew Christopher reminded everyone, "Do you remember when Nick had his hair dyed red and yellow and blue and orange. I told him, 'What happened to you? Did you get attacked by a gang of clowns?' Nick came back with, 'Well, what about when you had your hair parted on the side and everything below the part was shaved off and what little hair you had left was dyed bleach blonde?'"

"Yes, I remember that," Christopher laughed. "Uncle Steve asked me if I ran out of money at the barber shop."

Nick said, "Uncle Steve asked me, 'What happened to you? Did you lose a bet?'"

Their uncle said, "That is why I am here, boys—to point out to you when you do something stupid."

My niece Cherish added this story, "I remember when Angela was getting married. It was that big day before the big day, you know, picking out the wedding gown. My mother and I went to help her choose. She had it narrowed down to four gowns and she tried them on one at a time for us. We did the obligatory 'oohhs' and 'aahhhs.' But when she came out in her last gown, she looked stunning. Mom started to cry. Angela got upset and said, 'What is the matter? I thought you would like this one.'

"I said to Angela, 'No, dummy. That *is* the one she likes." Then they start hugging and crying all over each other and I'm like, 'Okay, are we done now? Can we go eat?'"

Mom offered up a story about Stephanie. "Steph, when you were little, your family came to visit me in Phoenix. We were at a restaurant and you were tired and started to get fussy, so your Mom picked you up to take you outside so you can walk around outside while we waited for the food. You looked at us and said, 'Don't worry, I'll be back.' I thought I was going to die laughing."

But nothing made Mom laugh more than hearing the stories about Sara. Annette said, "I remember when Sara was about ten and she had to do a school project on Heritage. She brought in the Zaccari Coat of Arms. As she explained to the class what the pictures meant, one boy asked, 'Why is that guy talking to the fish?' She answered, 'If you don't stop asking stupid questions, you will be sleeping with the fish,' a line she remembered from *The Godfather*. Her teacher said, 'There is no such thing as a stupid question,' so Sara said, 'Well there is now!'"

Mom had heard all these stories many times, but she laughed again and said, "I love you all." Her eyes were a little moist, but she had a big smile on her face as she looked around the room at everyone. Her gaze stopped on her sister. "Mary, go home get some sleep." Aunt Mary reassured her that she was feeling fine.

"No, really, Mary, why don't you go home and get some rest."

"Carm, I am not leaving you."

Then Mom said, "Mary, if you die before me, I'm going to kick your ass."

Aunt Mary shot back, "What are you trying to say, do I look like death warmed over?"

"Well. Now that you mention it, yes, you do," Mom smirked.

Aunt Mary returned with a remark in Italian, that when translated means "Go chase yourself with a sharp stick," and they both laugh like they have a thousand times in the past. Aunt Mary then jokes with all her great-nieces and great-nephews "See your grandmother? I come to see her and she gives me crap." This had the whole room in laughter.

The conversation and stories went on for well over two hours. Mom engaged everyone the entire time. It was as if they were all together for a holiday celebration rather than quietly awaiting death in a hospital.

Each grandchild came one at a time to hug her and say what they thought would be their final private words. Mom had a unique message and ended her words with, "Stay close to your parents; listen to your parents," to each grandchild, except Frank's daughters Stephanie and Sara. Mom's words to them were, "Stay close to your father; listen to your father." I thought this was unusual, but forty-five days later, we learned that Frank's wife had left their family. Although Frank had not mentioned any problems in his marriage, it was as if Mom knew what was about to happen. She knew her children and grandchildren so well that her loving instincts prepared them for challenges even before they happened.

Back at the house, Tony, Penny, and Leah prepared to make pizza for dinner. Uncle Tony asked Leah, "What do you think should be the first step to making a great pizza?"

Leah jumped up and down with excitement, and said, "Put the sauce on the pizza!"

"That's not the first thing."

Penny, who works in restaurant management for a large hotel chain, said, "Wash our hands."

Tony answered again, "No that is the second thing. The first thing is to get into the right mood." He dug through the CD collection and played Dean Martin's song, "That's Amore." Then the odd little trio—the slightly balding Italian guy; his blonde haired, blue eyed wife; and the little China doll danced the *tarantella* (an Italian wedding dance) in the living room. They laughed and cracked open a bottle of Welch's grape juice and drank it out of a wine glasses. As they were in the middle of mass-producing pizzas, the conversation became serious.

Little Leah asked, "Is Grandma going to die?"

Tony told her, "Yes, pretty soon Grandma is going to go to heaven to be with her little baby." Leah gave him a puzzled look and he continued. "When I was little like you, Grandma was going to have a baby, and something happened and the baby died and went to heaven. Do you know how the stars shine down on us at night? Well, the baby is up in heaven looking down at us just like the stars are shining down on us. Pretty soon Grandma will be up in heaven looking down at us. We won't be able to see her, but she will be able to see us. We can talk to her and she will hear us and we will be able to hear her too, but not with our ears. We will be able to hear her with our heart. She will be that little voice inside of you, reminding you how much she loves you."

"But I am still sad, Uncle Tony!"

"I know, sweetheart. I am sad, too, but I am happy that Grandma and her little baby are going to be together."

"Are we almost done making pizza?"

"Not yet. We are going to make four pizzas because Aunt Mary Anne, Nick, Chris, and Karen will be here soon, but now it's time for a break." Tony turned to Penny, "Maestro, if you would please."

Penny replayed the song again and they all left the kitchen singing, "When the moon hits your eye like a big pizza pie, that's amore."

My sister Mary Anne, her sons Nick and Chris, and Chris's wife of two months, Karen, walked into the house during Tony's explanation to Leah. Karen asked, "Did Grandma lose a baby?"

"Yes," said Mary Anne. "It was a long time ago. I was in seventh grade. Frank had just started high school. Tony, Annette, and Steve were still little. I think Steve was just five."

"What happened?" Karen asked.

"Mom had gone in for her annual physical when the doctor suggested a consultation with a surgeon. The doctor believed she might have a tumor in her colon. Since school was about to start, Mom decided to wait until the Christmas break when we were all out of school so Frank and I could help out with the younger ones. In the meantime she had become pregnant. So in early September, Mom went back to the doctor who confirmed she was pregnant. Mom told him she never went to the surgeon that he had suggested. So the doctor examined her again. This time he scheduled an appointment with the surgeon. Because she was pregnant, the surgeon did not want to do a signoidescope because he was fearful he would disturb the baby in the first trimester. A second surgeon was consulted. They all agreed that a scope test was needed now. On September 25, Mom answered the phone and heard, 'Hello, Carm, this is the doctor's office. Your lab results are in and the doctor would like to have a consultation with you immediately,' then there was a pause before the caller said, 'and could you bring your husband?' The words landed like a kick to the stomach. Mom felt her knees give out and she sank into the chair."

By this time, my cousin Kathy and her two daughters, Frank's daughters, Tony's daughters, and Dewey's daughter Nicole had arrived from the hospital. Kathy and Frank's daughters had never heard the whole story, so Mary Anne continued now with a houseful of people hanging on her every word.

"Sitting in the doctor's office, Mom and Dad were prepared for the worst. The doctors walked in and said, 'I will get right to it. Carm, you are four months pregnant. You also have colon cancer.' Mom felt tears well up in her eyes.

"Dad asked, 'So what are our options?' The doctors said they had consulted with another surgeon who suggested they force labor to abort the baby, let the uterus rest a while, and then do the surgery for the cancer. Mom's long-time OB-GYN doctor knew she would not agree to this. He contacted our parish priest and got the church's feeling on this matter. The doctor was right—Mom would not let them deliberately kill the baby.

"The doctors continued, 'To do radiation would certainly harm the baby. If we operate, there is chance that both of you could survive, but it is a very slim chance; maybe a one in a thousand chance. We have no medical precedence for your situation.' His next words were every couple's greatest nightmare. 'If we have to chose which one of you to save, what do you want us to do?'

"Mom did not even hesitate. She said, 'The baby.'

"The doctor said, 'Are you sure? You have five young children at home that need a mother.'

"Mom glared at the doctor and repeated, 'You save my baby. I would give my life for any of my children, including this one.'

"The doctor turned to Dad and asked, 'What do you think?'

"Dad also did not have to give it a second thought. 'You heard her; save the baby.'

"The doctor said to Dad, 'This will leave you the only parent to six children all under the age of fourteen. Are you sure?'

"Dad said, 'I don't know how I will do it, but I will. Somehow we will make it.'

"'What if we just wait and see if I can get through this pregnancy?' Mom asked.

"'If you try to go to term, you and the baby will die.'

"Our local surgeon was honest and said this surgery was too complex for him. So the doctors contacted Dr. Glenn Leak, a cancer specialist, and he agreed to do the surgery at Buffalo General Hospital. So Mom and Dad met with Dr. Leak and scheduled the surgery for October 10."

We were running out of Kleenex boxes at this point. Chris asked, "What happened next?"

Mary Anne continued, "I remember seeing a deep sorrow in Mom and Dad's eyes when they came home. I knew something was wrong, but I didn't know what. Later that night, after we had all gone to bed, Father Bernardo, the pastor at Holy Trinity Church came to the house. My brother

Frank was awake and sitting at the top of the stairs. No one could see him or knew he was listening. Father Bernardo said, 'I heard about what happened at the doctors.'

"Mom said, 'It is an easy decision, Father. Killing the baby is abortion and I will go to hell. I would give my life for any of my children, including this one.'

"My brother will never forget the next words from Father Bernardo, which were, 'You are not going into this surgery with the intent to terminate this pregnancy. You are going in with the intent to save both your life and the baby. If you think God wants you to continue with this pregnancy without taking the necessary medical steps, then I have failed as your pastor. Carm, if you don't have this procedure, you *and* the baby will die. Do you think God wants your five children to grow up without a mother? Intent is the key. The only hope for either of your survival is this surgery. Your intent is to save the child and yourself. There is a chance neither of you will survive this surgery. If the baby dies and you survive, it is *not* abortion.'

"Both Mom and Dad started to cry. Mom said, sobbing, 'We have been taught our whole life that given the choice, save the baby.'

"Father Bernardo replied, 'Carm, we worship a kind and loving God, not a cruel and heartless God. I want you to understand the difference. It is all about your intent, and your intentions are all good. This is not abortion. The doctors will do the very best they can, but there are no guarantees. Rest assured that regardless of what occurs, I will be there to make sure the baby is baptized and I will take care of all the costs if the baby dies.'

"As we waited the next two weeks for the surgery, we all knew something serious was about to occur. Mom and Dad tried to downplay the matter, telling us Mom has to go in for a minor procedure, but nearly every time Mom looked at one of us, she started to tear up."

Frank's daughter Stephanie said, "Oh my God, I can't even imagine going through something so terrible." Everyone is the house was now in tears, but all wanted Mary Anne to continue.

"The October morning Mom went to the hospital, she sent the five of us to school as always, but this time it was different. She hugged us all a little longer and tearfully said she loved us. She told us that she would not be there when we came home, but Grandma Mancuso would be there. She said what she thought might be her last goodbye. She stood on the front porch and watched us until we were out of sight. I know this because when I turned around, she was still waving to us with Grandma by her side."

Tony pulled out a letter and said, "Mom had written a journal about the events at the hospital. Let me read you her words."

The morning of October 10 Dad, Aunt Mary, and Aunt Ceta were walking in while I was being wheeled up to surgery. There was only a minute to talk. I told Dad, "I am not afraid. I had prayed that our children would be cared for and I was at peace." I didn't think I would live through the surgery and I was ready for whatever God had in store.

I was given a hypodermic shot and left in the hall near the surgery room to give it time to work. I can remember a Doctor coming to me calling my name—I was very relaxed and he said, "Hypo working very well." I remember being wheeled into the operating room where this man asked me my name, age, number of children I have, their names and my weight.

When I got to weight I said, "170–175, I don't know." At that point I felt myself go under. While I was in surgery, these are the things I experienced. I have never mentioned them to anyone for fear people would think I lost my mind. I remember a bright light coming toward me. I seemed to be in a dark place, the light was very bright and it did not hurt to look at it. I heard a warm reassuring voice that comforted me. I felt very content and at peace.

It was almost what some people call an out of body experience. It felt as if I was up by the ceiling looking down on the surgery. As I looked down I could see men in green hospital wear with caps and masks. They flipped me over on to my stomach and I felt the thread pulling through my skin as they sewed me up.

I remember the men were talking about the game, the World Series that they were listening to on a radio.

I heard Dr. Leak say, "Gentlemen, we worked very well together." I remember I thought of my five children and then I was down from the ceiling and back on the table.

I remember thinking I wanted the doctors to know I was able to hear them so I thought I would move my arm but nothing moved. I tried to move my leg and nothing again so I tried moving my head. I heard someone say, "She's waking up," and they put something on my nose and I was out again.

The next thing I remember was feeling someone standing near me. I was praying. One voice said, "What is she saying?"

The other person put their ear close to my lips and said, "She's praying."

Then this voice said, "We have to take her back because they left a sponge in her."

My first question to Dr. Leak in the recovery room was, "How is my baby?" He told me that the baby did not make it.

I remember screaming, "I told you to save my baby, not me!"

The doctor reassured me, "My dear friend, I would have respected your wishes, but as soon as we started we realized the baby was not alive. The baby was baptized as I promised."

The next thing I remember was my husband at my bedside. I told him they were bringing me back because they left a sponge in me. He told me that they already did that and I was back. I looked at him with overwhelming sorrow and said, "We lost our baby."

Trying to hold back his tears he said, "I know." From then on I prayed and thought about the baby and that I would like it buried back home. I looked at my husband. Losing this baby was the greatest sorrow we have ever experienced.

At this point Tony said to the house full of teary family members, "Let's take a break and eat some pizza." Tony and Penny cut up the pizzas; Nicole found some paper plates and Kathy's daughters Megan and Kristin poured some wine and sodas.

The break allowed everyone to regain their composure, and then Kristin said to Tony, "So tell us the rest of the story."

Tony said, "We all stayed home with Grandma and many other family and friends and waited for news. It was late when Dad came home. I saw sadness in his eyes that I had never seen before although he tried to smile for our sake. His voiced sound funny. All he could say was, 'The operation was a success, but we lost the baby.' We all started to cry, but Dad said, 'It's going to be okay. We are going to be okay. Mom is going to be in the hospital for several more days. She is going to be fine. We'll all go visit her this Sunday. Grandma would stay with us the entire time Mom was in the hospital. Having lost four children of her own and now losing a grandchild had to be devastating for her, but she set aside her grief to tend to our needs. Let me read you more from Mom's journal."

> The next day while in the Intensive Care Unit I kept thinking that I wanted my baby buried at home and not put into an incinerator. I didn't know what to do or how to begin having this done. If I could only talk to Father Bernardo, he could help. I felt a hand rest on mine. I opened my eyes and there stood Father Bernardo and Dr. Anthony Federico, an old family friend of the Zaccari's. I told Father Bernardo of my concern for my baby and he said he would take care of it and that I should not worry. Our baby was buried at Holy Trinity Cemetery after the 7 a.m. Mass. Dad had the baby in a vacuum-sealed plastic bag covered with a towel in a shoebox. Dad, Charlie Messina (the church janitor), Father William Lamphear (the assistant pastor), and Aunt Mary Crea were at the cemetery when my baby was buried. The grave is marked with a small stone that simply reads, "Baby Zaccari 1967". Father Lamphear said to my sister Mary, "Someday this child will come to bring her mother to heaven."

Tony said, "Mom wrote this next section just before Chris and Karen's wedding two months ago."

I was thirty-five years old when this happened. I am seventy-seven now with a failing heart valve. I know my time is coming soon. Since my experience in the operating room so many years ago, I was not and am not afraid of dying. I was so disappointed to find myself alive in the recovery room so long ago. I was so happy when I was with the light and with the voice. I didn't want to leave. At that moment I was completely at peace.

I am not afraid to die now, as I was not afraid then. I was concerned for my five children then. Now I am concerned for my son Steve. The "puzzle" is not completed yet. I pray no other pieces of my puzzle will bring unhappiness or suffering to those I love. We have all suffered enough!

Chapter 7:

Superman Can't Die

On Tuesday morning, September 22, the long line of visitors continued. Our cousins Dolores (Dee-Dee) Farina-Queen, her sister Mary Farina-Moore, and Mary's daughter Danette came to visit. When my brother Frank and sister Mary Anne were young, we used to live next door to Dee-Dee and Mary. Aunt Nina, their mother, was Grandma Zaccari's sister. Aunt Nina's husband Uncle Al was both Dad's and my brother Frank's confirmation sponsor. Aunt Nina's hair had turned completely white at a very early age. She always told the funniest stories and had a laugh like the comedian Phyllis Diller. You always heard Aunt Nina before you saw her. They also had two sons, Bobby, the oldest child, and Tommy, who died shortly after birth. The story came full circle many years later when Mary and Danette lived across the street from my parents' house.

Mary and Dee-Dee were particularly close to my mother. They would talk to her about dating, boyfriends, and life in general. They would also babysit when Mom had to get out of the house. On this Tuesday morning, it was girl talk day. The guys left and all of Mom's granddaughters, daughters, and Aunt Mary (who never left the hospital) were in the room. You could hear the laughter half way down the hallway. When Mom fell asleep about noon, most of the immediate family, along with Mary, Dee-Dee, and Danette, went to my parents' house to eat. Family and friends were delivering enough food to feed a small nation.

After Mary, Dee-Dee, and Danette left, Frank's daughter Stephanie asked, "What is the story about Bobby? When his name came up at the hospital, everyone became very emotional." My brother Tony told all the grandchildren the story.

"Bobby Farina ruled the neighborhood. He was the undisputed leader of Franklin Ave. Bobby was incredibly athletic, but didn't play sports in school. He looked somewhat like Frankie Avalon, you know the guy that sang 'Beauty School Dropout' in the movie *Grease*. Bobby was Uncle Frank's hero. To him, Bobby was Superman. Although Frank was only five or six, Bobby would always include him. Frank would often go next door when Bobby had friends over. Bobby and his friends would be playing the old 45 rpm records, singing, dancing, using the couch as a fake piano, and playing air guitar. Sometimes Bobby and his friend would stand at the corner store and sing 1950s songs. While his friends weren't too crazy about this little boy hanging out, no one dared to challenge Bobby.

"Frank used to say, 'Bobby could throw a ball so high in the air, it would reach heaven.' Frank could always tell a good story. Frank, Mary, and Dee-Dee used to play outside most days. Aunt Nina had three very large horse chestnut trees. One of their favorite things was to collect horse chestnuts and throw them at the train boxcars across the street. There was a guy from the next block who would walk down Franklin Ave. and tease them. He would take their ball or whatever they were playing with, and when they protested he would throw it across the street onto the railroad tracks. Frank would try to punch the guy, but he was only six or seven. The guy would just laugh and push Frank to the ground. One day Frank told Bobby what was happening. Bobby said, 'Don't worry about it. You keep doing what you are doing. Don't run away from this guy. I'll take care of everything.' A few days later, the guy comes walking down the street. At first Frank, Mary, and Dee-Dee wanted to run into the house, but he remembered what Bobby said and stood their ground. The guy started to tease them again, but this time Bobby jumped out of one of the trees and landed right in front of the guy. Bobby grabbed the guy by the shirt and said, 'So you think you are a tough guy, picking on girls and a little boy? Let's see how tough you are.' The guy tried to run, but Bobby smacked him in the face a couple times and told him, 'I don't ever want to hear that you walked down this street again.' Frank couldn't stay out of the confrontation. He yelled at the guy, 'Yeah, don't ever come back,' and kicked him in the shin. According the Mary and Dee-Dee, they never saw this guy on their block again."

Everyone laughed. Stephanie said, "I can see my Dad doing that."

"When we were little, we used to live upstairs from my Grandma Zaccari. Your grandma used to lock the keys in the house every now and then. She would call Bobby and he would climb from the downstairs porch and pull himself onto the upstairs porch where were lived. As he would climb up, he would pretend to slip and just hang on with one hand just to make your grandmother crazy. That would make Uncle Frank say, 'Bobby is Superman.'"

Tony continued, "When Bobby was about eighteen, he and some friends enlisted in the Navy. They would get in their uniforms and walk to the Navy reserve meetings until he left for active duty. It was a big event when Bobby would come home on leave. One time he came home with a convertible Chevrolet. He gave everyone in the neighborhood a ride, but he gave Frank a private ride around the lake and let him wear his Navy hat."

"During that visit Grandma introduced Bobby to her niece Angie LaPlaca. Angie was Grandma's sister Lucy's daughter. It was love at first sight. Even though Bobby was stationed in California, he would come home as often as he could to see Angie. It wasn't long before Bobby and Angie were engaged. Bobby was planning to re-enlist. The plan was to transfer to a base on the East Coast to be closer to home. Everyone was thrilled, especially Uncle Frank. Bobby, his hero, his Superman, was going to marry Angie, his favorite female cousin. The family was counting down the days to the wedding."

At that point my brother Frank walked into the house. Sara said, "Dad, Uncle Tony has been telling us about Bobby Farina."

"Good, I want to hear this, too."

Tony said, "I got to the point where Bobby and Angie were planning to get married. Why don't you finish this; you know it better than me."

Frank continued the story. "Bobby went back to California, and a few weeks later we received a call that he had been in a very serious car accident. The police pronounced him dead at the scene, but when he started to moan and move, they rushed him to the hospital. After some emergency surgery and a long recovery, Bobby was fine. He came back home to visit after the accident and all the talk was about the wedding. Everyone was excited.

"Because of the accident, Bobby couldn't do sea duty, so he was stationed near El Centro, California, until he got his strength back and could return to sea duty. I was in third or fourth grade. It was just before Halloween, around October 28. I remember Grandma coming into my room early in the morning before school. She was crying hysterically and said, 'Bobby is dead.' I jumped right out of the bed and said, 'No, he's not. He's OK now after the car accident.' Grandma kept crying and said, 'There was an air show at his base and a plane crashed into the building where he was working. He's dead.'" At that point, Frank's eyes swelled with tears. This happened nearly fifty years ago and it still makes him cry.

Tony, seeing the tears in Frank's eyes, stepped in and said, "I remember walking into the funeral home with Dad, Mom, Frank, and Mary Anne. There were flowers everywhere. There was a flag-draped coffin with a picture of Bobby in his Navy uniform. When your grandmother saw the coffin, she fainted. Grandpa caught her, and Uncle Joe and Grandpa took her outside for some air. I was so young that I didn't know what was going on and started to cry. Angie came over and took Mary Anne and me out to the garden. I asked her, 'Why are you and my Mom and everyone crying?' She said, 'We are all sad, but I am happy now that you are here.' I was still confused, but I remember feeling better."

Frank regained his composure and continued, "The Navy sent his body home for burial. It was a full military funeral. I told Father Bernardo I had to be one of the altar boys for this funeral. He approved and I carried the cross, which was probably a mistake. At a Catholic funeral, the cross bearer goes down with the priest to meet the casket as it is removed from the hearse. The casket was covered with an American flag and was carried by six Navy pallbearers. The priest waited for most of the immediate family to enter the back of the church. So I stood there and watched all our relatives walk into the church. Aunt Nina was nearly catatonic. She couldn't even stand up. Uncle Al and Grandpa had to help her into the church. It was one of the saddest moments of my life. After the funeral, we all went to the cemetery. The Navy honor guard folded the flag and handed it to Aunt Nina. The officer who handed her the flag said something like, 'Please accept this flag with the condolences and gratitude of a grateful nation.' Then a military trumpeter played 'Taps' and there was a three-gun salute. Everyone lost it as soon as they started to play 'Taps.' I kept looking from Aunt Nina to Angie. The sorrow was overwhelming. I kept saying to myself, "*Bobby is Superman. Superman can't die.*"

Tony's daughter Cherish said, "That is such a sad story. No wonder everyone got teary at the hospital."

Tony said, "The rest of us (Mary Anne, Annette, Steve, and I) were too young to understand what was happening. We asked Frank, 'What happened to Bobby?' Frank told us, 'Bobby went up to heaven to get his ball back.' It made us feel better. Your Uncle Frank always protected us. He always made us feel better."

After lunch we all headed back to the hospital.

Chapter 8:

Italian Grandparents, Holidays, Traditions, and Curses

Mom was awake, but looked considerably weaker when we returned. Our cousin Paul Nasca visited the hospital. Paul was one of five brothers. His mother, Mary, was Dad's sister. Ever notice how Italian families keep recycling names? In this family we had Aunt Mary Crea, Aunt Mary Nasca, Mary Anne, and Annette Marie. Then there was Kristen, Sandra's daughter, and Kristin, Kathy's daughter; Sara Pieszak and Sara Zaccari; Stephanie Zaccari and Stefanie Crea. Not to be left out were Frank (Dad), Frank (my brother), and Frank Crea.

After a few minutes, the stories turned to family, holidays, traditions, and curses. Our grandfathers died before we were born, so we learned our history, traditions, and stories from our grandmothers. They were very different in appearance, mannerism, and personalities, but they were the same when it came to their grandchildren. Their grandchildren were their life, and even God could not help anyone who even considered doing something to hurt their grandchildren.

Grandma Zaccari

Grandma Zaccari was the stereotypical Italian grandmother. She was short, on the heavy side, talked a mile a minute, had an opinion on every topic and was not shy to make sure everyone knew what that opinion was. In fact, one joke around the family was that if Grandma wants your opinion, she will give one to you. She was involved in every church organization, loved to win (particularly at the card game pinochle), and ruled as the supreme matriarch of her family. She had five children and twenty-two grandchildren, all living within a few blocks of each other.

Our families got together for every holiday and nearly every weekend in the summer. Summer weekends were water skiing, picnics, and playing some game that involved cards or a ball. The major card games were: cribbage, where my Father and Uncle Joe Griffo held a godlike status; seven and a half, a modified version of blackjack that all the cousins played for pennies every Christmas eve; and pinochle, my grandmother's game.

My grandmother would play pinochle nearly every day, be it on her breaks at work, at her church events, or at family gatherings. The cards would come out shortly after the meal, and they would play for hours. The games were like marathons. Pinochle is a poor man's bridge. It took four to play, two per team. There was bidding for potential points; you had to follow suit or you could trump if you were out of a particular suit. The idea was for your team to win the most tricks. Teams kept score. The first team to fifteen-hundred points won.

The players were usually Grandma, Uncle Joe, my father, and Uncle Pete, unless my father or Uncle Pete could hide until another victim was recruited. Once the grandchildren got close to our teens, we were recruited to play. My grandmother usually won. She had a secret weapon—she cheated, but she was so good at it no one realized what was happening. Grandma was diabetic and had trouble seeing the cards "when it was convenient for her," per Uncle Joe.

Grandma would not always follow suit, but given the frivolity around the card table, no one paid much attention. Paul and Frank, who were the same age, did notice once in a while, but said nothing. They figured out how to make money playing pinochle against their school friends by developing a few subtle hand signs. They became very good.

One holiday Paul and Frank were playing against Grandma and one of our other cousins. Paul and Frank were cleaning up; they must have won four or five games in a row. Grandma, being so competitive, replaced one partner with another, then another, but Paul and Frank kept winning. Finally at one point, Frank scratched his ear, which was not one of the signs. Paul played a card, Grandma beat his card, and then Frank trumped her card. At that point, Grandma had enough, threw the cards across the room, and yelled, "Paul and Frank cheat!" This made the entire house erupt in laughter.

Uncle Joe said, "What's the matter, Grandma, do they cheat better than you?" "This brought more laughter. For the rest of her life, whenever the cards came out to play Grandma would announce "I'm not playing with Paul and Frank, because they cheat!" I will let you in on a little secret -all my cousins cheat when we play cards.

Christmas Eve

Christmas Eve was our all-time favorite event. We would rotate houses for each holiday, but Christmas Eve was always at my parents' house. We would bring in long cafeteria-like tables and everyone had to bring folding chairs to accommodate everyone. It was like a Norman Rockwell scene if he was Italian. Picture this: twenty-two children, five sets of parents, and Grandma Zaccari. There was more food than you can image plus a huge Christmas tree and gifts for everyone. We almost needed an extension to the house to hold everything and everyone.

For many years Catholics didn't eat meat on Christmas Eve, so many Italians would do the seven fishes meal. We, however, didn't do that. Grandma would try to make a squid thing, but it was terrible. All the grandchildren didn't have to eat it, since we were children and the Pope wanted children to eat something. It was amazing how many aunts and uncles volunteered to help the grandchildren and then eat with us to avoid the squid. Once the Pope lifted the no meat ban, Christmas Eve meals became legendary. The meal would start with spaghetti or lasagna, and many times both. Of course there were meatballs and Italian sausage. Then chicken or turkey, ham, and every side dish you can imagine. Then of course there was salad, fruit, and nuts (Italians eat salad last). The desserts looked like a scene from the Food Network show *Cake Boss*. There were several cakes, waffle cookies (pizzelle), fig cookies (cucidati), and cannoli. We learned at a very early age that a homemade cannoli is so rich, you can only eat one a year at Christmas, or you will have a heart attack and die on the spot.

We didn't have just a meal; we had a feast. The kitchen was the sole domain of my mother, my aunts, and my grandmother. They all made sure everyone knew how much time and effort it took to produce such an amazing spread. They would complain about how tired they were or that they would appreciate a little help, but anyone who dared to enter the kitchen was quickly and often loudly dismissed. The Italian comedian Mike Marino does a routine about his Italian mother that describes the holiday meal perfectly. To paraphrase Mike Marino:

> My mother had one job, and that was to make food everyday for fifty people. They weren't there, but she

made it just in case someone came over. At every holiday she would say the same thing—"I'm getting too old to do all this cooking. One of you better learn how to make this meal, because I am getting too old and too tired. In fact you tell your Uncle Joe to take a picture of all of you eating because this is the last time I'm cooking." Next holiday someone would try to help and my mother would throw them out of the kitchen. In fact I believe it was one of my very early female relatives who is responsible for the painting of the Last Supper. I bet it went something like this: "Jesus Christ, come here, I want to talk to you about something. First put your hair in a pony tail and put on some sandals, you know I hate it when you dress like that. You know, Jesus, your apostles don't appreciate all the food I make for them. I'm getting too old for this. One of your apostles needs to take a turn and cook. I'll tell you what; this is the last time I'm doing this. In fact, you call your friend Leonardo de Vinci and tell him to paint a picture of all of you eating my food, because I'm not doing this anymore. This is The Last Supper."

Clearly, Mike Marino is 100 percent Italian.

After our meal (which took quite a while), there was a gift exchange, general family conversation, then pinochle until 10:00 p.m., when Grandma would announce that someone had to take her to church so she could get a good seat for midnight mass. It's ten o'clock. Midnight mass starts at midnight, but it didn't matter; someone had to drive and go with Grandma at ten. The selection was between one of Grandma's children. My father and his brothers and sisters would draw straws or cut cards, or roll dice or make a cash bribe to determine the "lucky one" that would sit at the church for two hours before mass starts and then two more hours for midnight mass. The more rational people would head over to midnight mass shortly before midnight. The ones who did not go to midnight mass would take the homemade rolls out of the freezer and start to cook Italian sausage so everyone could eat after midnight mass. People would get back to the house after mass about 2:00 a.m. and the feast would start again. Finally about four in the morning, the party would break up. There was nothing like Christmas Eve.

The Curse

No one can recall the year, but our most memorable Christmas Eve involved "The Curse." Grandma Z boasted that she had twenty-two grandchildren, while no one in her church or work social groups had more than six. In fact, she said, "I have more grandchildren than all the women at my last card party combined." For those of you not familiar with the grandchildren phenomenon, here is the story. Italian grandmothers believe their place in heaven in based on the size of their family. The theory is that if God blessed you with many children, then in God's eyes, you were a particularly important person. God would watch over you and if He felt you were an exceptionally good person, He would send more children your way. After all, God would not give you more of his children to care for if you were a loser. You have to remember, there wasn't much sex education being taught back then!

Grandma Z figured since she had five children and they produced twenty-two grandchildren, then by her math (four children minimum per grandchild), she should have eighty-eight great-grandchildren, and three-hundred-fifty-two great-great-grandchildren, and so on. Grandma Z would have family tree so large that her place in heaven would be next to God Himself. Given how much Grandma liked to win, we all thought if she was that close to the throne, she might bump God over and keep the throne herself.

One of my female cousins said, "No way Grandma. I'm not having four kids. I just want two a boy and a girl."

To which Grandma replied, "You get how many God sends you. You don't have a say in the matter."

"Oh, yes, we do. It's called birth control." The instant we heard those words, we all braced ourselves for the volcanic eruption that was about to occur. Grandma's face got so red that we thought her head was going to explode.

She slammed her hands on the table and stood up and yelled, "You people (whenever she was real upset, *you people* were always the first two words) can't practice birth control. It's a sin. You'll all go to hell, and I am not about to have that black mark on my record. So you all just want one boy and one girl. Well, as of this moment, I put a curse on all my grandchildren. Your first two children will be the same sex. Now if you want a boy and a girl, you will have to have three children. How do you like that?" My cousin knew enough to just back away. If she didn't, her twenty-one other cousins would have pulled her into another room. Grandma continued to vent, "There is no way Mrs. LaTona is going to have more great-grandchildren then me. Oh, she would just love that." Then with a wave of her arm she said, "You are all cursed." Aunt Mary then intervened and started to get Grandma ready to leave for midnight Mass.

After Grandma left for Mass, all the cousins got together and started to laugh. My brother Frank said, "Can you believe that? She put a curse on us. I think Grandma has finally lost it." Everyone laughed and thought this will be a good story to tell the next generation. None of us took her curse seriously. Eighteen of her twenty-two grandchildren became parents. In every case, they had two boys or two girls. After the third or fourth occurrence, my cousins with one child all started to panic. Whenever they would find out if one of us was pregnant with a second child, the phone calls would start. When they found out Frank was going to have a second child, he received the phone calls. "Find out the sex of that baby," they would insist. His response was, "I don't care. I just want a healthy baby." "Well, find out and let us know because we are thinking of having a second child, but someone has to break the curse first." I am here to tell you, *never, ever* laugh at a curse from a full-bloodied Italian grandmother. My cousin Phil finally broke the curse. But by the time he had children, the rest of us were long done with having babies. Grandma won. The curse worked. I can hear her laughing in heaven.

"Do you remember Grandma's funeral?" Tony added, "She died on October 19, 1978. Grandma always said the first grandson from each family were to serve as her pallbearers. Frank was in California in the military. Dad called to tell him that Grandma had died. Frank said he would contact the Red Cross for an emergency leave, but Dad said it's not necessary to fly across the country for the funeral. With Frank in California, I was next in line to be one of the pallbearers. During the church service, while Father Bernardo was eulogizing Grandma, a light bulb above the pallbearers flickered and then fell out of its socket. It hit Carl on the shoulder, bounced off and hit Peter on the knee and then fell to the floor between all of us and sat there for a second and a half, and then exploded, showering us all with glass. No one was hurt, but everyone speculated on what this meant. Someone suggested that Grandma was telling Father Bernardo to hurry up. (He could be a little long-winded.) Maybe it was a message to Frank for not coming. No one knew for sure, but I just assumed we had not heard the last from Grandma."

Grandma Mancuso

Grandma Mancuso was very different. She was small in stature, soft-spoken, and carried herself with a regal presence. She spoke with a very heavy accent, but when she spoke, everyone listened. As we mentioned earlier, she left Sicily at age fifteen to move to American to care for her late sister's children and marry my grandfather, a man she had never met, who was once her brother-in-law. Grandma Mancuso lived a very hard life. She raised twelve children and buried four; had thirty-one grandchildren, and too many great-grandchildren to count. She worked on farms and canning factories most of her life, yet none of her grandchildren can ever recall hearing her complain. We never heard any "poor me" or "I never got a break" stories. She was fiercely proud and independent. Mary Anne once asked Grandma why she never remarried. Grandma's response, "One husband is enough, and sometimes that is too many."

Both of our grandmothers were always there when needed. Grandma Zaccari spent a great deal of time helping her daughter Mary raise five boys under the age of ten after Uncle Carl died. Between our mother and her sister Mary, Grandma Mancuso had eleven grandchildren that lived within two blocks of each other, so we saw Grandma Mancuso more than Grandma Zaccari.

The best way to honor someone is to listen and pass on the stories about their life. Grandma Mancuso had many funny stories.

Steve often says, "A few things I remember about Grandma Mancuso are that she would say, 'Don't make foolish to me' (meaning not to make fun of her). She said about Aunt Lucy and Mom that they would still be making 'foolish' twenty years after she died." Well, Grandma, it has been thirty-six years since you died, and your family is still telling stories about you.

Tony said, "She used to like to watch championship wrestling with my brother Frank when he was little (before it became the WWE stuff you see now). There was a wrestler named 'The Beast' who supposedly was from Sicily. The man worn a loincloth, had unruly hair and beard, and was the single hairiest man on the planet. He was made out to be the villain, so the wrestling promoters had him win many times to build up interest. Grandma used to tell us 'That's a no true,' (meaning Sicilian men don't act and dress like that). Grandma hated The Beast. She would always stay in the background and act like she wasn't watching, but she wanted to see this guy lose. The day finally came when The Beast was losing; she jumped up and yelled, 'Get him!' My cousins and I turned and looked at her in shock. When we told her wrestling is all fake, she didn't believe us. She didn't believe the moon landing really happened, but she believed wresting was real."

Aunt Mary Crea tells a story about the nicknames Grandpa gave to Grandma: "The Fireman" and "El Postino" (The Postman). She wore a housecoat, but underneath she was always dressed and ready at a moment's notice. She didn't drive, but loved to travel. She would just take off her housecoat; leave it on the table, and go. Grandpa would see the housecoat on the table when he got home and tell the kids, "The fireman must have gone out today." The Postman nickname came because Grandma had to stop and talk at everyone's house on the way home from church or the store. Grandpa and the rest of the family would continue walking home and Grandpa would tell the kids, "That El Postino was out making her rounds." My brother Steve inherited the El Postino gene, because he cannot go anywhere where he doesn't know 99 percent of the people in the room. My sister Annette calls him 'the mayor,' because it takes Steve more than an hour to leave every event.

Aunt Mary recalled that Grandma once took the bus and train from New York to California to visit some relatives when my brother Frank was a baby. She didn't speak very good English but found her relatives without getting lost. One Sunday she called her house to talk to her children. When they asked her how long she was going to stay, she said, "Maybe another month."

At that point Mom, who had just had her first baby, started to cry and said, "No, Mom! Come home! I need your help." Grandma was on the next plane home.

Annette tells a story about how Mary Anne and Grandma used to tease each other. Mary Anne was ruthless. Whenever we played any kind of game, she was out to win at all costs. She was also not a gracious winner. Grandma would watch us plan Monopoly and, as usual, Mary Anne was winning and gloating. Grandma would steal money from Mary Anne and put it in the cardboard roll, the ones you get from paper towels, and throw it to us when Mary Anne wasn't looking.

Grandma Mancuso could put together a seven-course meal in what seemed to be minutes. The food was amazing, with one exception: Grandma thought oregano was a topping for pizza. To this day we have never seen another green pizza.

Tony tells a story about Grandma's ability to instantly produce a meal. "I remember one time just after my older brother Frank got his driver license, my Mother told him to go pick up Grandma and bring her to our house for dinner. Steve and I went with him and I think my grandmother was shocked to see us. She of course invited us in, hugged and kissed us, and two minutes later, there was hot pizza and pound cake on the table. This was before the invention of the microwave oven. I really don't know how she cooked it so fast. While we were eating, she started to fry up some homemade Italian sausage with peppers and onions, plus a small side of rigatoni noodles and homemade sauce. Then Frank finally remembered why we were there and said to Grandma, 'We are here to bring you to our house for dinner.' My grandmother, who was standing there in her house coat and slippers, just took off her house coat to reveal her dress underneath. She went into the other room for ten seconds, came back with her shoes on, her purse, and said, 'OK, let's go.'"

While Grandma Mancuso loved all her grandchildren, my brother Frank was her favorite. When Frank was born, Dad was working on the railroad. He would leave on Sunday and not return until Friday night. Mom, who was only twenty-one and alone with a new baby, would take Frank to see Grandma nearly every day. The two formed a very special bond. Whenever Frank came home from college or on leave from the military, one of his first stops in the morning was to see Grandma. He would drop Mom and the rest of the family off at school, and then drive to Grandma's house. She knew he was coming and always had a feast prepared. They would eat and talk for hours. I recall when Grandma was near death. She looked so tired and exhausted, then Frank, who had come home on leave from the Air Force, walked in and Grandma sat right up smiled for the first time in days. They sat and talked until Grandma finally fell asleep, but that night was different. She didn't look tired and exhausted. She looked happy and at peace.

What Our Grandparents Saw

Like most second-generation Italian-Americans, our grandparents came to America in the early 1900s. In less than a hundred years, they saw the world change. Tony wrote this note on Thanksgiving Day 2010.

> As with most holidays, I spend some time thinking about my grandparents. They were born in the late 1800s through the early 1900s. I have fond memories of my grandmothers. Both died in the 1970s. On Christmas 2006, I loaded up the car and the family and drove down the New York State Thruway from Rochester to Buffalo. My two daughters Angela and Cherish sat in the back seat with my son-in-law David.

They watched a movie on the DVD being played on David's new laptop. My wife, Penny, sat with me in the front seat and talked to her sister Dawn on a cell phone. I drove and listened to a Christmas CD. When we arrived at my sister Mary Anne's house, I asked everyone this question: "If someone told our grandparents, when they were traveling on a boat from Italy to Ellis Island, that someday their grandchildren and great-grandchildren would travel with the conveniences we have today, what would they say?"

The answers came quickly; my daughters and nephews said, "They would ask, 'What's a CD, DVD, cell phone, and laptop?'"

Mary Anne said, "No, they would ask, 'What's a movie?'"

My mother said, "No, they would ask, 'What is a car?'"

Then my father put it all into perspective. "No, the first question would be, 'What is a highway?'" There were no highways when they arrived in America. The roads were not paved. They drove a horse and buggy over dirt roads. We often speak of the past generation as the ones who paved the way for how we live today. Our grandparents literally built and paved the roads. They built the railroads and the first cars, airplanes, radios, televisions, and the factories. None of these things existed when they arrived at Ellis Island with simply a hope for a better life.

I have much to be thankful for this Thanksgiving. I have the treasure of a loving family and friends, those still in my life, and those who paved the way for us. Happy Thanksgiving!

The Wisdom of our Grandfathers

Both of our Grandfathers died in the mid-1940s. Even though they lived within three miles of each other, they never met. They never shared a glass of wine or a meal together. They never shared stories about the old country together. But my parents independently told us a story they often heard from both of my grandfathers that are hauntingly similar. Both parables are cautionary tales about how we need to respect the elderly. Since they never met, I can only assume this characteristic is deeply woven into the fabric of Italian families.

My mother's story went like this:

There was an elderly man who lived with this son and grandson. The elderly man was sickly and becoming difficult to live with, so the son told the grandson, "Put Grandpa on the old cart and wheel him way out into the wilderness. After he falls asleep, leave him on the cart with some water and food and then walk back home." About four hours later, the grandson came back home pushing the empty cart. His father said to him, "I told you to leave that old cart with Grandpa."

The son replied, "I was going to, but then I figured that we are going to need it again someday."

My father's story was similar:

An elderly man lived with his son's family. When the father became too sick to care for anymore, the son carried his father into the woods. When he came to a little meadow he told his father, "I have to rest for a minute, so I am going to put you down here."

The father replied, "Yes, put me down here. This is the same spot where I rested with my father."

What goes around comes around.

The Memories

Our grandmothers always made us feel they had been waiting all day just to see us, and now their day was complete. The thing we most remember about our grandmothers was the love. Their love was total, complete, and unconditional. They were the counterbalance to the day-to-day family struggles. They knew when and how to let our parents know to back off without challenging their authority. They let us do things our parents might frown upon, like staying up late, eating leftover pizza for breakfast, putting hot chocolate milk on breakfast cereal, or bringing her granddaughters breakfast in bed. As my sister Annette said on many occasions, "It would be a cold day in hell before Mom or Aunt Mary would bring their daughters breakfast in bed."

They talked with their grandsons about what it means to be a real man, to love your wife, and how to provide for and care for a family. They listened to our side of an argument with our parents and were able to help us understand our parents' point of view without being condescending or autocratic.

More importantly they would sit and talk for hours with their granddaughters about life, sex, marriage, and how to be a good woman, a caring wife and loving mother, sharing family secrets and recipes. There were no cookbooks. Nothing was written down. Our grandmothers showed us how to cook, how to make spaghetti sauce, meatballs, and all the great Italian meals and desserts. They showed us how to feed a family of seven for a week with nothing but various types of beans and noodles. They showed us what needs to be done to feed, raise, and love your family, because at the end of the day all you have is family.

Our cousin Sandra once said, "We didn't learn the important lessons in life by reading books or watching a TV show. We learned by doing it together. It was these moments of sharing and doing where we learned how to run a household and that as women we are the lifeblood of the family."

Her sister Kathy once said, "What I learned from being with Grandma was as a wife and mother, I create and maintain the tone for my family. I learned that the greatest responsibility I have is to provide a safe and happy home."

So if your grandparents are alive, enjoy them, cherish them, and listen to their stories. Learn how your family came to be. Make great memories with them. If your grandparents are gone, never forget those memories and make sure you tell your grandchildren about the trials and sacrifices your grandparents made so they could live in this great country and never ever take it for granted.

Chapter 9:

A Real Love Story

The procession of friends and relatives continued all day Tuesday. Tuesday evening, Frank and Dewey brought Italian sandwiches to the hospital. While Dad, Frank, Aunt Mary, and Mary Anne stayed with Mom and the current visitors, Tony, Dewey, and Annette took everyone down to the hospital break room to eat. While they were eating, Tony's daughter Cherish said, "Grandma and Grandpa have been married fifty-seven years. That is hard to believe these days."

Tony said, "The line in a wedding ceremony, 'til death to us part' was very real to our grandparents and parents. That line meant total and complete commitment to each other and their family. It meant no matter what happened, no matter what heartache, no matter how hard times were—and there were many very hard times—they held on to each other, they pulled together, and weathered the storm. This is not to say they lived a 'Pollyanna' type of life. They lived in the real world and went through some incredible hardship, but divorce was never an option. Grandma Mancuso would often say, 'Most Italian marriages are made in heaven…right next to where they make thunder and lightning.' Something my mother used to say whenever a friend of hers confided they were contemplating divorce was, 'I never once considered divorcing my husband. Kill him, yes; but never divorce.' This always made her friend smile and often gave her the strength to continue to make the marriage work."

As I mentioned earlier, my mother and father met at the announcement dinner shortly before the wedding of my father's first cousin Sam Crea and my mother's sister Mary Mancuso. They were both in the wedding party on November 24, 1950. (Uncle Sam and Aunt Mary have been married more than sixty years.) When Mom first met Dad, it wasn't exactly love at first sight. She thought to herself, "What an ugly suit. That guy looks terrible in brown."

Dad, on the other hand, went for the charm approach. He asked her how old she was, and when she said, "I am seventeen," Dad called her a liar and said that she looked much older. Needless to say, they didn't leave the wedding reception together.

After the wedding, Dad did not call Mom for several months. When he finally got around to calling, he had to remind her how they met. Mom's response was, "Oh yes, the guy in the ugly brown suit who called me a liar…yes, I remember you." Dad had to do some fancy maneuvering, but Mom reluctantly agreed to meet. The next day, however, she had second thoughts and was going to break the date when he called back. However, realizing he had dodged a bullet, Dad never called back to confirm. He just showed up at the agreed-on time and they went on a date.

But after that rocky start, a true love story began. My brother Tony tells his daughters, "You can fall in love, and you can also fall in cow manure. Love is choice. Falling in cow manure is an accident. Love is not an accident. Choose to be in love everyday. Work at being and staying in love everyday." That is what my parents did; they chose love. Sure, they had their ups and downs, but whenever they were faced with a make-or-break decision, they chose love.

My father is an easy-going kind of guy; however, he does have strong feelings for four things: God, family, his country, and the Buffalo Bills. To this day you could still get a frustrated growl out of him if you mention Super Bowl XXV, XXVI, XXVII, or XXVIII, especially the wide right field goal attempt in Super Bowl XXV. Most other things he was pretty neutral about, although playing cribbage and a good dish of pasta sugo (for you non-Italians, that's spaghetti and meatballs) could bring a smile to his face. But what he really liked doing was getting out on a dance floor, especially to the big band groups like Glenn Miller and Tommy Dorsey. Once they started dating, my parents would go to a dance hall or to someone's house that had a record player and dance the night away. My mother would tell us this story. One day my Dad bought a record, *Tenderly* by Ray Anthony, and since neither owned a phonograph, they were taking it to friend's house. Before they got there, Dad dropped the record and it broke. They were the old hard vinyl records that played at 78 rpms. Dad was devastated. It took a couple of weeks before he could afford to buy *Tenderly* again, and once again it broke on the way to a friend's house. The third time, he carried the record carefully under his arm. Just before he and my mother arrived at the place where they were going to play the record, someone accidentally bumped into Dad and the record cracked in half again. This time Dad started jumping up and down on the record. My mother said that at first she stood there in stunned silence. Then they just calmly walked away. When they got about a half a block away, they just both looked at each other and just started laughing. It was the turning point in their relationship. Mom had seen Dad at his worst and decided his best far outweighed his worst.

Fifty-four years later, at the wedding of their granddaughter Angela, the bride and groom decided to do an anniversary dance. The DJ asked all the married couples to dance on the floor. Then the DJ asked everyone who was married less than a year to please leave the floor. After a short while, the DJ asked everyone married less than five years to leave the floor. They continued to ask for everyone married less than ten years, then fifteen years, then twenty years, until there was just Mom and Dad left on the floor. Then David, the groom, nodded to the DJ, and without missing a beat, the song was changed almost without anyone noticing. So while Ray Anthony sang, "As the evening breeze caressed the trees tenderly," Mom and Dad danced with each other. Few people attending the reception that day realized the significance of that moment and no one, including my mother and my father, knew that would be the last time they would dance together—well, at least in this life.

This love story lasted fifty-seven years. Can you image that today? A couple married fifty-seven years and more in love after all those years than the day they were married.

The love story between Carm and Frank Zaccari continues. My father, now eighty-one, still lives in the old family home. He visits Mom's grave site every week. He cleans off the head stone, plants new flowers, and tells the only woman he ever loved how things are going with their children, grandchildren, and now great-grandchildren.

It is my greatest wish that everyone who reads this book has a love story like my mother and father.

Chapter 10:

You Will Graduate from College if It Kills Us Both

"When you look into your mother's eyes, you know that is the purest love you can find on this earth."

—Mitch Albom, *For One More Day*

Late Tuesday night, Mom was talking to Annette and said, "I haven't always been the best daughter, the best daughter-in-law, the best sister, or the best sister-in-law. I haven't always been the best wife, the best mother or mother-in-law, but right now, I feel nothing but forgiveness to everyone who has ever done anything to hurt me and I hope that they forgive me, too." She paused for a moment, the silence hung heavy in the air, and then she continued, "I hope I was a good mother to you."

Annette replied, "I just hope and pray that I am half the mother you are."

Mom smiled with appreciation. "I'm sure you will be. Leah is so well adjusted and she is so smart. Tell my little China doll and all my grandchildren that I expect great things from them. Tell them to pay attention in school and—" Annette finished the sentence with Mom, "keep their brains open." Everyone in the room laughed.

We heard that line every single day from kindergarten until we left for college. There was no discussion about *if* we were going to college. We all knew we had no choice. This point was driven home when my brother Frank was a sophomore in high school. He was a pretty good baseball player and his dream was to play for the New York Yankees. He was struggling with geometry and made the unfortunate mistake of saying to Mom, "I don't know why I have to learn this crap, since I am going to sign a baseball contract right out of high school." Everything and everyone stopped what they were doing and ran for cover.

Mom stood up and looked at Frank with fire coming out of her eyes and said in a tone of voice that nearly shook the house, "*You will graduate from college if it kills us both.*" She then turned to the rest of us, her face still red, body shaking, and said, "And that goes for the rest of you!"

Education was the be-all and end-all for Mom. She wasn't able to graduate from high school. She dropped out when Grandma Mancuso was injured on the job and couldn't work. At first Aunt Mary said she would drop out and get a job to support the family, but Mom said, "No,

Mary, you only have one year left. You finish. I'll get a job and go back to school when Ma is better." To this very day, Aunt Mary's eyes fill with tears when she talks about this decision. Mom did plan to go back to school, but life had other plans. Once she started working, the family needed her income, and she never went back to high school.

One would never know she didn't finish high school when you saw how actively and aggressively Mom helped all of us with homework. She was determined to see that we all attended high academic Catholic schools through high school. Mom and Dad did not let their tight financial situation deter us from a first-class education. Mom ironed the altar linens at the church for years in return for tuition. She was a fixture at every school event and fundraiser. Dad worked bingo every week for as long as we can remember to help offset our tuition costs. We all saw how much our parents sacrificed for our education, and after the outburst with Frank, we made sure we did our best in school.

Not finishing high school was something that haunted Mom. When Frank started his junior year in high school, Mom began to work on her GED. Having been out of school for more than twenty years did not deter her one bit. She stayed up late every night and enlisted the help of Aunt Mary, and before Frank completed his junior year, Mom was awarded with her GED diploma. We all remember how proud she was, and we were all proud of her. We had a little celebration meal with the Creas. Aunt Mary started to cry when Mom showed her the diploma. Aunt

Mary kept saying, "Thank you so much for what you did so many years ago."

Mom whispered back, "I did what needed to be done. It's over now. I have my diploma." Mom then turned to her five children and six nieces and nephews and said, "You see, it is never too late to get your education. Never forget this," as all eleven of us said with her, "You will graduate from college if it kills us both." Everyone laughed, but we all knew Mom was serious.

Shortly after Frank left for college, Mom became the secretary at Holy Trinity School. It was a job she kept for more than twenty-five years. When Father Bernardo hired her, he said, "There is no one who better represents the commitment and dedication to education than Carm Zaccari." Mom was far more than a secretary. She was more like Radar O'Reilly from the television show *M.A.S.H.* She did whatever was needed. She helped out in the classrooms, during lunch periods, recess, and after school. She did the banking and often would drop off schoolwork to the parents whose children were sick or injured so they didn't fall further behind. Without question, her most important role at Holy Trinity was the moral support and constant encouragement she offered to struggling students and new teachers.

The great poet Maya Angelou once said, "You can only become truly accomplished at something you love. Don't make money your goal. Instead, pursue the things you love doing, and do them so well that people can't take their eyes off you."

Tony leaned toward his daughter Cherish and said, "Like I have told you all your life, it doesn't matter what you do for a living. Do it the best you can every day."

Steve was ready to head back to the hotel. He said to Mom, "You did pretty well for someone who didn't finish high school. All of us not only graduated from college, but graduated with honors. That's quite a legacy.""

Mary Anne started to laugh and said, "I think we were all too scared not to go to college."

Mom said, "Make damn sure that my grandchildren and great-grandchildren go to college, or I will come back and haunt all of you."

Steve said, "I would laugh, except I saw what happened when we laughed at Grandma Zaccari's curse."

Chapter 11:

The Beginning of the End

After Frank took Steve to the hotel, he returned to the hospital to join Mary Anne, Annette, Tony, Dad, and Aunt Mary. Late Tuesday night and early Wednesday morning, things started to change for the worse. Mom started to complain about a shooting pain in her foot. She said the blanket was hurting her foot. We lifted the blanket off her foot and Mary Anne went to tell the nurse to increase the IV drip. A few minutes later, a nurse came in and increased the flow but it did not help. Mom continued to complain about pain. She was sweating profusely and thrashing in the bed. Mary Anne and Annette went back to talk to the nurse. Mary Anne called Angela, Tony's daughter, a professor at the School of Pharmacy at St. John Fisher and a practicing pharmacist.

In layman's terms, Angela said Mom needed a bridge drug to be given via the IV for the short-term pain, and then the morphine drip should be increased to a level higher than the level of the previous pain medication.

Being a nurse, Mary Anne understood what Angela said and told the nurse to call Dr. Helen so we could discuss this recommendation. The nurse initially refused by referring to the doctor's orders, which did not specify the steps Angela suggested. Annette glared at the nurse and said, "I'm sorry, you have your PhD in pharmacy from *which* university?" The nurse was taken back. Annette continued, "Either you call the doctor, or we are going to drive to her house." The flustered nurse called Dr. Helen to complain about these unruly visitors. When Dr. Helen was on the phone, Mary Anne took the phone from the nurse and said, "Helen, this is Mary Anne." She then explained Angela's recommendation. Dr. Helen agreed and gave a verbal order to the nurse. At this point the nurse was both frustrated and totally confused.

You could see her thinking, "Who are these people?" Mary Anne, who always had the last word as a kid, said, "I'm sorry to step on your toes, but don't screw with us when it concerns my mother's treatment. Helen and I grew up together. My mother was like her second mother growing up."

There were no further issues with the hospital staff. My sisters' actions reinforced the long-standing belief that two things you do not mess with are Italian women when the issue involves a family member and a Grizzly bear with cubs. My father often said, "Having lived with Italian women all my life, I'd rather take my chances with the bear."

Angela's recommendation worked as described, and Mom finally fell into a deep sleep. We all looked at each other and knew it would be a matter of hours. Dr. Helen came by in the morning and talked with my sisters and father. There was nothing to do but wait.

Wednesday morning, Mom's brother Marion came to the hospital with his wife and grandson. All of my immediate family and the grandchildren were also present along with Aunt Mary, her daughters Kathy and Sandra, and Mom's niece Susan. Mom went back and forth from being awake and asleep. When awake, she would talk to each person in the room and wanted them to come to the bed so she could hug them. It was just a matter of time.

Mom reached up for Dad and said, "Sara's here. Open the door."

Dad thought she was asking for Frank's daughter Sara, and said, "Sara is right here, Carm."

"No, open the door; Sara Pieszak is trying to come in."

Annette opened the door and said, "OK, Mom, Sara can come in now."

Mom said, "She's here…she's here."

Aunt Mary stepped up to the bed and said, "Carm, do you see Ma?"

"Yes, yes, she is right here with Sara and me. I see Pa, too."

"How is it there, Carm?" Aunt Mary continued.

"It is so beautiful."

Mom then looked at Dad and said, "I love you. Don't be sad or afraid. I am going to be OK. Sara is bringing me my baby. I see my baby. I am holding her hand!" When we heard this, there were tears in everyone's eyes as we remembered the words of Father Lamphear, "Someday this child will come to bring her mother to heaven."

"I am holding our baby, Frank; I'm holding Christine. She is so beautiful." Mom relaxed for several minutes. The grandchildren's eyes were as wide as saucers.

My brother Frank said to them, "Don't be afraid. This is something that I have seen many times when people are about to die. They see their relatives who have passed before them. The Italians believe that your family members come down to escort you into to heaven."

Nick asked, "Is Grandma hallucinating?"

Frank said, "Some people will say it is just hallucinations, but I saw many people die in the military, and if it is a hallucination, then in every case where I was present, the dying people are having the exact same hallucination. Maybe it's not hallucinations; maybe it's real. I guess we'll find out when it is our time."

Mary Anne was standing next to the bed. Mom opened her eyes and said, "Is Concetta here?"

"No, Mom, Aunt Ceta isn't here."

"Get her. We have to talk. Grandma Zaccari said we have to end this thing and forgive."

Frank said, "Mom, Aunt Ceta's not here. Just say what you need to say, and we will get the message to her."

"No. Grandma Zaccari said we need to forgive. Find her."

Annette called our cousin Jenny, Aunt Ceta's daughter. Annette explained the situation, and that Mom was dying. Jenny said she was on her way to her mother's house and would call as soon as she arrived. A few minutes later, Annette's cell phone rang. "Annette, this is Jenny. I have my mother." Annette explained the situation to Aunt Ceta. They were both crying.

We could hear Aunt Ceta saying, "I am so sorry. Your mother needs to be concerned about your dad and you kids, not me." She then paused and said, "Leave it to my mother to reach out from the grave to make peace." Annette then held the phone next to Mom's ear and they both settled whatever feud had existed.

Tony said, "I knew we hadn't heard the last from Grandma Zaccari when that light bulb fell during her funeral."

Mom then squeezed Dad's hand and said, "It's done. All is finally forgiven. Sara and Christine, I'm ready."

Dad then said to her, "Carm, we got the paper that the lien has been released on the house." Ten years ago, my parents received a government grant to upgrade their home. The deal was that if they sold the house within ten years, they would owe a prorated amount of the grant. If they stayed in the house, the grant would be forgiven. Dad had just received the official release in the mail.

Mom squeezed his hand and said, "Thank God. That takes care of the last detail."

Mom looked peaceful after talking with Aunt Ceta. The furrows on her forehead that knitted her eyebrow together seem to erase before our eyes. The ever-present knot in her stomach that made her look uncomfortable was gone. Even the air seemed to tremble with the sound of a sustained violin vibrato. Time seemed to slow to a crawl in that moment as our collective mind joined together as one. We looked around the room at each other as if to say, "Are you seeing what I am seeing?"

Even Mary Anne's taciturn husband Myron said, "Whoa that was intense."

My mother's deep brown eyes seem to take on a bluish hue. She closed her eyes and went to sleep.

Tony remembers a conversation he had with Mom two weeks earlier. She had just been rushed to the hospital because she could not breathe. "The next day she told me, 'I don't know why I am still here. I thought last night was going to finally be the end.' I told her, 'Well, Mom, there must be something that you still have to do here.' She said, 'What? What *else can* there possibly be left to do?'"

Tony shrugged his shoulders and said, "'I don't know, Mom, but I am sure we will find out.' Do you think this was it? Is this what has been keeping her tethered to this life? Guilt? Remorse? Forgiveness?"

Penny whispered to her daughters, nieces, and nephews, "This is why we tell you to forgive and move on with your life. It's not healthy to carry a grudge." No one said a word, but the look in everyone's eyes said we had just witnessed something very profound.

Finally Steve leaned over in his wheelchair toward Tony and said, "I am sorry for all the times that I have called you a douche bag."

Tony chuckled and said, "You called me a douche bag this morning at the hotel."

"Yeah, I guess I did. Then I'm sorry for all the times except for this morning, because you were a douche bag." And with that, the spell that everyone seemed to be under broke, and everyone in the room exhaled.

Frank, Tony, and Dewey went to the local grocery store to pick up some precooked chickens and brought all the grandchildren to the break room to eat. Angela explained to her cousins what was going to happen from this point. "Grandma will go in and out of a very deep sleep. She will go deeper into a coma. She will get what is called the 'death rattle' as she breathes. Eventually her organs will start to shut down, and she will die peacefully. It won't be much longer."

Frank asked Tony, "What is the deal between Mom and Aunt Ceta? How long has this been going on?"

"It started the day you were born. You remember the old Italian tradition that the best man is the godfather and the maid of honor is the godmother for the first child, right? Uncle Phil was the best man and your godfather. Well, Aunt Ceta was Mom's maid of honor because Aunt Mary had just had a baby a few days before the wedding. When Mom announced that Aunt Lucy would be your godmother, the feud was on."

"Are you kidding me? This has been going on for fifty-six years?"

Tony said, "You know how Sicilians can hold a grudge."

After they ate, Angela, her husband David, and Chris and his wife Karen took their cousins to visit Ron Nasca's pottery shop in Fredonia. (He was another cousin.) They just seemed to know that the grandchildren needed a break.

Back in the room, there was a long period of silence. Everyone was sitting quietly, lost in their own thoughts, exhausted by the ordeal and what we just witnessed. Mom opened her eyes and looked around. She was too weak to talk. My brother Tony walked up to her and said, "What was that, Mom?" He put his ear closer to her and said, "Did you just say that I was always your favorite?" He waited, pretending that she was answering, and then added, "You did?! I knew it!" He announced, "Sorry, guys, but it looks like I was always her favorite." My mother just shook her head and smiled in amusement. "But I do have a serious question for you, Mom; do you think Amish people go camping? I was just wondering." Mom weakly snickered and gives him the backhanded, get-the-hell-out-of-here wave of her hand. "How about this one: If you are wearing a pedometer and you walk backwards, will it subtract your steps?"

My father laughed and asked, "Where the hell do you come up with these things?"

Steve answered, "Tony's mind is a strange place."

Tony's wife muttered, "Ain't that the truth." We all laughed. It seemed like old times.

Chapter 12:

Life with Integrity

After a short visit and a pottery-making lesson at Cousin Ron's shop, the grandchildren all headed over my parents' house. As the oldest grandchild, Angela took out what had to be sixty photo albums and told her cousins, "We are going to make a collage for the funeral. In fact we are going to make several. One will be photos of just Grandma and Grandpa. We'll make one highlighting each of our parents, so we need pictures of each one with Grandpa or Grandma. Another collage will just be us the grandchildren, and, finally, one with Grandma and her parents, brothers, and sisters." She gave several photo albums to each cousin and assigned each a task. "Pull out the pictures you like, and I will handle the design and production."

So the cousins started going through all the albums. Frank's daughter Stephanie found the album that we gave Dad for his eightieth birthday. All the cousins stopped what they were doing and went through the album together. Everyone in the family had written Dad a note. There were pictures of all the major events in his life. When they came to the page with the family crest, they all looked to Angela for an explanation.

Angela explained that Dad's father, Grandpa Zaccari, was known for his integrity. Integrity is doing what is right because, and only because, it is the right thing to do. So across the bottom of the coat of arms is the family motto: "Life with Integrity."

And that is exactly what it means, life with integrity. No exceptions, no excuses. Live your life with integrity, period.

"Uncle Frank's letter was amazing," said Nick. "Grandpa started to get choked up when Uncle Frank read the letter."

"Your Dad really gave a nice talk," Angela told Stephanie and Sara, who weren't able to make it to the eightieth birthday party. "He started his talk by saying, 'Dad, this was going to be your eulogy, but you lived too long.'" Stephanie then read the letter out loud.

> Years ago one of our ancestors decided Life with Integrity would be the Zaccari family motto. To show us what Life with Integrity means, God sent us Frank Zaccari. Here is some of what Life with Integrity means.
>
> In 1967 mom was diagnosed with colon cancer. She was also pregnant. Medical history at that time said NO ONE had ever survived this combination. Dad had to prepare himself to not only lose his wife, but to raise

five children under the age of fourteen. Through God's grace, Mom survived. During this ordeal, I never once heard Dad complain, "Why me" to God. He was ready to do whatever it took. That's Frank Zaccari, and that's Life with Integrity.

In 1970 it appeared Cardinal Mindszenty High School was going to close. Dad led a group of parents who helped raise the money through donations and bingo to keep the school open another nine years until Steve graduated. He worked bingo every week for over a decade. That's Frank Zaccari, and that's Life with Integrity.

In 1972, I was home from college and picked Dad up from work at Excelco in Silver Creek. I arrived a few minutes before 4:00. At exactly 4:00 a number of men walked out of the building, but Dad was not one of them. I walked over where I could see that he stopped his machine at 4:00, walked over to "punch out," then washed up to go home. When I asked why the other guys were all walking out the door at 4:00 yet he kept on working until 4:00, he told me something I will never forget. "I get paid to work from eight to four. That means I start working at eight and stop at four. They don't pay me to get coffee at eight or to clean up at 3:30." That's Frank Zaccari and that's Life with Integrity.

In 1985 our family suffered through our greatest challenge, the terrible accident that nearly killed Steve and resulted in his paralysis. We were all devastated, afraid, and angry, yet Dad never complained or lamented, "Why did this happen to us?" He was prepared to deal with the situation no matter what it took. That's Frank Zaccari and that's Life with Integrity.

In his retirement Dad continues to stay involved with Challenger Sports Program for disabled children, bingo, and caretaker at Steve's house every year. He doesn't expect any praise or accolades—he does what he believes is right. That's Frank Zaccari and that's Life with Integrity.

When I talk to my children, nieces, nephews, and now great-nephew, I tell them to do the best they can and do the right thing. If you ever have any question or doubt about what is right, just do what your grandfather would have done and you will be OK. That's Frank Zaccari (you know what's coming, so say it with me) and that's Life with Integrity.

"Wow," said Karen, "What a powerful statement." It is a powerful statement and it is something my family believes in and does its very best to live by each day.

Cherish said, "I wrote a paper for a sociology class about our family coat of arms. I remember writing that words mean nothing if they are not followed up by actions. My grandfather is someone that I try to model my life after because he has lived by this motto his whole life."

"Grandpa never says much," said Sara. "Maybe that's because Grandma is always talking." All the cousins laughed.

Angela said, "Grandpa is the most honorable man we will ever know. My Dad used to tell us after Grandma came home for her cancer surgery, Grandpa did the laundry, often cooked meals, and made sure everyone got to where they needed to be for school and sport activities. He didn't just do these things until Grandma got better. He always did them. That was very unusual for an Italian man back in those days. Most of the men expected to go to work and then be waited on when they got home. Very few ever helped out with the kids or around the house. Grandpa was a man ahead of his time."

"What a great role model for his sons," said Stephanie. "My Dad is like that, too. He usually cooks the meals, does the laundry, and a great deal of the cleaning around the house."

Cherish added, "Our Dad is the same way. I hear my friends and their mothers complain that the fathers don't ever help out around the house."

"Now you know what kind of man to look for when you start thinking of getting married," Angela added.

"Is that what you did?" Sara asked.

"David is a very involved parent and does many things around the house. If I hadn't grown up watching Grandpa and our fathers, I would have never known there are men who are like them. I dated some guys that expected to be waited on, but those relationships didn't last very long. Those types of guys can be fun to date, but there is no way you want to share your life or raise a family together."

Angela had the attention of all her cousins now, so she continued, "When Uncle Frank was born, Grandpa worked on the railroad. He was the track supervisor responsible for maintaining the entire New York Central track from Buffalo to Ashtabula Ohio. That was a big job. He would leave on a train every Sunday night and come back every Friday. So Grandma was alone with Uncle Frank during the week. Grandpa had seniority, was paid well, and was very well respected. When Aunt Mary Anne was born, he told Grandma, I have to find another job. I can't be gone all week now that we have a daughter." The brought a chorus of "Aww" from all the female cousins.

"Is that when he started working as a machinist on the space program rockets?" Nick asked.

"Yes, that is when he went to work at Excelco. At first he didn't make as much money as the railroad, but it was more important to him to stop traveling. The first few years he worked from 4:30 p.m. to 11:30 p.m. All the kids would get home from school about 3:00, eat dinner with

Grandpa, and then he would go to work. About the time Uncle Frank was starting high school; Grandpa was working the day shift and could attend all the after-school events."

"That sounds so much like my Dad," Sara said. "He was a corporate CEO for many years, but he used to travel quite frequently. When Stephanie was about to start high school, he got out of the high-tech world and bought the insurance agency so he would stop traveling all the time. He made less money but wanted to be involved in our lives. I bet he learned that from Grandpa."

Chris said, "We live the closest to Grandma and Grandpa, and I can honestly say I have never heard him complain about his life or being Grandma's caretaker as she was getting sicker, or what happened to Uncle Steve. Grandpa has been at the hospital with Grandma this entire week and hasn't complained once or said he's tired or anything. He's just there with Grandma and does what needs to be done."

Karen added, "Life with Integrity."

Nick said, "I heard Grandpa complain once. It was when Scott Norwood's last second field goal attempt went wide right and the Buffalo Bills lost the one Super Bowl they should have won." Everyone laughed.

"We all screamed when that happened," Chris said with disgust.

My sister Annette walked into the house to pick up some clothes for Leah who was staying with Kathy and her daughters. She commented on the progress of the collage and how impressed she was that all the cousins were doing this together. "Aunt Annette, how did Uncle Steve get hurt?" Karen asked. "I have heard parts of the story, but never the entire thing." Only Angela was old enough to remember Steve before the accident. Chris was just a baby, and none of the other cousins were even born when the accident occurred.

Annette sat down and told her nieces and nephews the story. "I was visiting Mom and Dad for the Mancuso family reunion. Steve called to say hello to everyone. The phone gets passed around so that everyone gets to say hello. Steve told us how much he loves his new job. He would travel to a store that was struggling and his team would do a complete remodel, which took about eight weeks. Then he would move to a new location and start again. I remember Tony asking him, 'And you like this?'

"Steve said, 'Well, the traveling is a difficult, but I have seemed to hit my stride when it comes time to do the actual job. Have you heard that new song my Matthew Wilder called "Ain't Nothing Gonna Break My Stride."' Tony told him 'No,' so Steve starts singing it:

> Ain't nothing going to break my stride
> Nobody's going to slow me down
> Oh no, I've got to keep on moving

> Ain't nothing going to break my stride
> I am running and I would not touch ground
> Oh no, I've got to keep on moving

"'That is my new theme song,' Steve said. Then he told us he was leaving for Delaware in about an hour.

"So after the reunion as we walked into the house, the phone rang. Grandpa answered the phone and nearly fell over. He looked completely white, like all the blood had been drained from his body. He just said, 'I don't understand this. I don't know what to do. Here, talk to my daughter,' and he handed me the phone. The caller was a doctor in New Jersey who asked me if I had a brother named Steven Zaccari.

"I said, 'Yes, what's wrong?' The doctor said Steve was involved in a very serious car accident. He was at the hospital and wanted me to call.

"I asked if he was alright and the doctor said, 'It was a very serious accident. He had to be extracted by the Jaws of Life and was transported to our hospital on the New Jersey, Delaware, and Pennsylvania border. He is in a great deal of pain and has no feeling in his arms and legs. We are getting X-rays now. Let me give you my name and phone number and I will call you once I see the X-rays.'"

Sara asked, "This is when you were running the Rehabilitation Hospital in New Jersey, right?"

"Yes, it was. I called Frank Crea, who was also in town for the Mancuso reunion. I told him what happened and asked him to help me locate the hospital. Frank lived near Philadelphia and was familiar with the area. Within ten minutes, Frank and Aunt Mary were at the door. When Mom opened the door, she and Aunt Mary embraced and sobbed. Dad looked like he was in shock. I told everyone we don't know what we are dealing with yet, so let's stay as calm as possible. I called my brother Frank in California but I was crying so hard all I could say was that Steve was in an accident. You all know how Uncle Frank just takes charge in a crisis." All the cousins just nodded. "Uncle Frank said, 'Is he alright?' All I could say was, 'No.' Then Uncle Frank asked, 'Is he dead?'"

"That's my dad—direct and to the point," said Stephanie.

"I gained my composure and told him no and gave Uncle Frank the doctor's name and phone number. He said, 'I will call the doctor right now. How are Mom and Dad?'

"'Not good!'

"Uncle Frank said, 'Keep everyone calm. I will call right back.'"

"You guys know Uncle Frank was a medic in the military and how forceful he can be when something involves his family, right?"

"Yeah, we saw him talk to one of the people at the hospital who wouldn't let one of the visitors go into Grandma's room," Nick said. "I almost felt sorry for the guy." This made everyone laugh.

"Uncle Frank called back in a few minutes and said, 'The doctor cannot see the sixth and seventh cervical vertebrates. While that is not good, it is too soon to tell the extent of the damage, but at the moment he has no feeling or movement from the chest down. It could just be from the trauma and swelling at the moment. The doctor will stabilize Steve and transfer him to Thomas Jefferson Hospital in Philadelphia. He said it was one of the best spinal cord trauma hospitals in the country. I told Uncle Frank I would make arrangement to take Mom and Dad to Philadelphia in the morning.

"As soon as Steve arrived at Thomas Jefferson, the doctor called the house. Mom went on the extension upstairs in her room and I was in the living room. Dad, Frank Crea, and Aunt Mary were next to me. The doctor told me Steve broke his neck at the C-6 C-7 vertebrae. I started to cry, as I knew what this would mean for Steve. He would be paralyzed from the chest down and all limbs were affected, including limited use of his hands. I knew from that moment what this meant for us all. Aunt Mary became alarmed when she saw me break down with the doctor and told Frank Crea, 'Run to Aunt Carm. Something bad is happening.' When I regained my composure, I discussed the treatment with the doctor. I asked him to tell Steve that we were on our way. Aunt Mary and Frank helped us pack all night. No sleeping for any of us. The next morning

Mom was finishing her packing. She and Dad had no idea how bad this was going to be.

"I told Mom she was going to see some things that would be frightening. I tried to explain what to expect and how bad this was, but she cut me off and yelled, 'Pray for a miracle then!' We drove to the Crea's house to borrow a suitcase. I was alone with Dianne (Aunt Mary's youngest child) and Aunt Mary. I told her what we were going to see when we arrived in Philly and I was afraid for Mom and Dad. We all embraced and cried. I felt like I was keeping a secret from everyone, knowing that Steve would be profoundly affected, but I knew I had to be strong in order to help Mom and Dad endure. Losing hope for Mom and Dad at that time was not an option. Uncle Sam gave Mom an envelope full of money.

"Mom told him, 'I promise you, Sam, that we will pay you back everything.'

"Uncle Sam said, 'Don't worry about it. Just let us know what else we can do.'

"The flight to Philly was the first time Grandpa had ever been on an airplane. His first plane ride was to see his injured son. I have only seen Grandpa cry three times in my life: when his brothers Phil and Pete died, and on that airplane. Grandma just kept rocking back and forth in the seat, praying the rosary."

Cherish said, "I can't imagine what Grandpa and Grandma were going through."

Annette continued, "I walked into Thomas Jefferson Hospital with Mom, Dad, and Frank Crea. Thank God Frank Crea was with us. I could not have dealt with the treatment plan and helped Mom and Dad without him. When we walked into the room and saw Steve in the striker frame bed, they all looked sick with worry. Steve tried to ease their concerns by rolling his hands around each other in front of himself and then threw one over his shoulder and then rolled them again and threw the other hand over the other shoulder like the famous samba dancer Carmen Miranda.

"'Doesn't anyone else want to dance?' he asked."

"Thomas Jefferson has dormitories where the family of a spinal cord patient can stay for a minimal fee. I believe it was ten dollars a night. My parents planned to stay until things stabilized. I met with the doctors and rehabilitation specialists. There was nothing to do until the spinal cord was stabilized. Then the doctors would perform surgery to fuse his vertebrate and place Steve in a halo. The halo is where screws are drilled into your head to hold a halo in place to prevent movement of the neck and spinal cord. The surgery was scheduled in two days. There was nothing to do but wait."

Annette continued, "So we waited. Not the strongest virtue of this family." Everyone laughed. "In then meantime, Uncle Frank was very busy. He wrote letters to Congressman Jack Kemp, to Lee Iacocca, then chairman of Chrysler, and New York Governor Mario Cuomo. He told them the story and asked if they could find time in their busy schedules to please write to Steve. Despite their extremely busy schedules, each one sent a very personal letter. Governor Cuomo even called and Jack Kemp visited Steve in the hospital. I can never thank them enough for their kindness and compassion.

"Then Uncle Frank called me and said to go to where the car had been towed and get pictures of Steve's car and the other cars that were involved. He told me to take several pictures from all sides and angles. Then he called a law firm in Philly and made an appointment to meet with the lawyer. Uncle Frank said, 'We are going to make sure Steve is protected and compensated.'"

"How did Uncle Frank know to do all that?" asked Nick.

"He just does," Sara answered. "He is good in a crisis; it's the little things that drive him crazy." That brought more laughter.

"Do you guys remember the woman that was with Uncle Steve at Chris and Karen's wedding two months ago?" Annette asked.

"Yeah," answered Chris, "He said her name was Joan."

"So who was she?" Angela asked.

"Joan and Uncle Steve had been dating. Depending on which story you believe, they either just got engaged or were planning to get engaged."

This brought a gasp of, "Oh my God" from all the cousins.

"What happened?" asked Karen.

"Well, Joan came to the hospital and stayed with us at dorms. By this time Uncle Tony, Aunt Mary Anne, and Uncle Frank had all arrived in Philly."

"The next day we learned the operation was as successful as possible and Steve would be wearing the halo for three months. The doctors told us it was not likely he would ever walk again. Best-case scenario was he could move his arms, but did not have control of his fingers. He would be wheelchair-bound for life as a quadriplegic. Now it was time for the doctors to tell Uncle Steve. We told the doctors that his support system was all here. The doctor asked Steve if he wanted a family member to sit in on the meeting. Joan assumed it would be her and started to get up. Steve said, 'I want my sister Annette. She is involved in long-term rehab and she will be able to help me understand.' So I went into the room with the doctors and Uncle Steve. Everyone else went to the waiting area until we came out."

Cherish said, "That had to be devastating for Joan?"

"I'm sure it was, but my concern at that moment was for my brother. The meeting with the doctors took about forty-five minutes. I put on my counselor hat and was very much involved in the treatment process. Afterward we all met and stayed with Uncle Steve until he was sedated and went to sleep. We were all devastated by the news and walked across the street to a little diner that Grandma and Grandpa stopped at every night. The diner staff had been so kind to Grandma and Grandpa. They could see the hurt and pain in their eyes the first night. All the waitresses and the owner talked with my parents and cried with them when they heard the story. They didn't charge my parent to eat and the owner would always stop at the Thomas Jefferson dorms on his way home to give my parents some food. I will never forget their kindness."

"That night back in the dormitory, I was filling the family in on the expected rehab. I explained all the tests and how long the expected stay would be at Jefferson then McGee Rehabilitation hospital. After the news, Joan asked Uncle Frank if she could talk to him privately. She told Uncle Frank how hurt she was that Steve had asked for me and not her. She said, 'I feel your family is pushing me out.' Uncle Frank told her she was very important in Uncle Steve's life and she could do things for him that we could not. He told her we are a very close family. All we had growing up was each other. When one of us is happy, we are all happy, and when one is hurting, we all 'circle the wagons' and protect. He told her this is a life-changing event. None of us will ever be the same. You are welcome to stay as long as you like.

You may be able to deal with this long term or not. If you do, that will be wonderful. However if you can't, no one in the family will hold that against you. There is one thing you have to understand. You may not always be his girlfriend, but he will always be our brother. Joan stayed around for about two years. Those first two years were very difficult for Uncle Steve. He was in and out of the hospital several times with infections and other surgeries. He once told me that he didn't expect to live five years, and he knew the life they had planned together was not going to happen but he wanted her to still have a chance at that life with someone else. We didn't see Joan again until the wedding twenty-two years later."

"Did they stay in touch over the years?" Stephanie asked.

"They stayed in touch off and on over the years. Joan got married and had two daughters and the life that they had always talked about having together. She's divorced now so she and Uncle Steve agreed to meet and talk at the wedding."

Nick said, "It looks like they had a good time together. Do you think they will try again?"

"Who knows?"

"My family met with the lawyer in Philly. Frank told them the story and our concern. The senior partner said they would be happy to represent Steve, but they felt there may be a case against the New Jersey Highway Department. He said if there is a case we won't charge you a dime. We will take a percentage of the settlement. Frank told them do what they needed to do and keep him posted."

Annette continued the story. "Uncle Steve was at Jefferson for about two months. He was transferred to McGee Rehabilitation hospital about four blocks from Jefferson for another four months. During one of my visits, a nurse asked me, 'Who is your brother? I mean, who is he really?' I asked her what she meant. She told me that when singer Teddy Pendergrass was a patient at Jefferson and McGee, he set the record for mail. 'Your brother has broken that record. Plus he gets letters from people like United States Senator Max Cleland, Governor of New York Mario Cuomo, and Congressman Jack Kemp, the mayor of Buffalo, a Catholic Cardinal, and Senator Ted Kennedy.' I told her my brother has a magic about him. Everyone who has ever met or spent time with him knows he is special. Even his friends from grade school and high school all stay in touch. His story and how he has accepted this terrible tragedy and how he is helping other patients in this hospital learn to deal with their tragedy has touched so many people."

Stephanie asked, "What was the deal with the trial?"

Annette continued, "Steve went to court twice. The first time was a battle over the worker compensation claim. The insurance company was fighting the claim. So Steve was in the hospital for six months, and when he was discharged he still didn't have his customized wheelchair. So he ended up in court. The judge was not happy and ordered the company to pay all his hospital bills, all medical supplies needed and for his medical care for the rest of his life. The also had to renovate at least one house for him and customize a van."

"The second time was the negligence trial with the New Jersey Highway Department."

Sara asked, "Was that the one with the chicken and the Sprite?"

Annette laughed and said, "Yes. Your Aunt Mary Anne had me laughing during the testimony. Grandpa just glared at us, but Aunt Mary Anne could not stop giggling. We had to walk out of the court room."

Karen asked, "What happened?"

At this point Mary Anne had joined Annette and the grandkids. Mary Anne continued the story. "The opposing lawyer, who sounded like Don Knots, asked Steve if he stopped to eat. Steve said yes. Then the lawyer asked, 'What did you eat?' Steve said, 'Chicken and Sprite.' Then this lawyer starts saying things like, 'Did you pay for the chicken and Sprite? Did you get reimbursed from the company for the chicken and Sprite? Was chicken and Sprite an approved meal? Why did you stop at that particular restaurant for the chicken and Sprite?' So it was like listening to Don Knots, you know, the guy that played Barney Fife, keep repeating chicken and Sprite, chicken and Sprite. It was like a bad episode of Andy Griffith and I just could not stop giggling."

Karen asked, "So how did the trial end up?"

"The judge strongly suggested that they settle with Steve, which they did. I never was told the exact amount, but the goal was for it to be enough for him to live on the rest of his life."

"Is that when he moved to Phoenix?" Cherish asked.

"First he finished his master's degree at Buffalo State University, and then he moved. He just could not stay here in Buffalo with all the snow in a wheel chair."

"So how did the two of you get to live right next door to each other?" Cherish asked.

Annette said, "I was living in Phoenix. The plan was to buy some property and then build two houses connected by a breezeway. Then the lady who lived next door to me died. She was eighty or ninety years old. So I went next door to visit the family who all lived in Minnesota. I told them how sorry I was and if they wanted me to keep an eye on the house. They said they were hoping to sell it quickly since they didn't want a house in Arizona. So I told them if they could wait forty-eight hours, my brother might buy this house. I told them about Uncle Steve and they said they would not only sell the house at a great price, but leave all the furniture. The house was a mirror image of mine. So I got my video camera and walked through the house and sent the tape to Steve. Since worker's compensation had to renovate a house for him anyway, Steve agreed to buy the house. I knew a contractor who had the exact same injury as Steve so he knew exactly what needed to be done. Once the renovations were close to done, Steve moved to Phoenix and we have lived next door ever since."

Chapter 13:

Reunion at Heaven's Gate

As Mom fell deeper into a coma, we all knew the end was near. Everyone was tired so we decided to start sleeping in shifts and Mary Anne and Tony went back to my parents' house to sleep. Tony slept in the living room and later talked about a dream he had that night. "Our grandmothers and many other deceased relatives were sitting in the living room. I saw Aunt Grace and Aunt Lucy. They turned to look at me and said, 'Don't worry about your mother. We have been waiting for her and will take good care of her.' They were sitting forward and smiling. They leaned back and I saw Sara Pieszak and my baby sister Christine walk in with Mom."

Father Lamphear was right. I did welcome my mother to heaven. While I never actually lived on earth, I was always part of my family. Mom made a birthday cake for me every year. She never said it was a birthday cake but my dad, brothers, and sisters all knew. There was a place set for me at my parents' fiftieth wedding anniversary and at every major family event. My spirit was with my family for many events. I rode in the ambulance that took my brother Steve to the hospital after his terrible accident. He thought he was going to die, but I assured him he would not and let him know there were many great things in store for him. I have been there for every major event in their lives: the weddings, births, divorces (sorry Frank), graduations, good times and bad. Now Mom and I will be looking out for our family together. By the way, guys, Mom said to keep your brains open; you haven't heard the last from her, either.

About 11:30 p.m., September 23, 2009, after more than twenty-five hours on their feet, my father, my brother Frank, my sister Annette, and my Aunt Mary Crea went home to sleep. Mary Anne and Tony took their place at my mother's bedside. As Mom slept Mary Anne and Tony sat on either sides of her bed and held her hand. They listened to Mom breathe; Mary Anne explained that the sound they heard was known as the death rattle. It sounded like a cross between snoring and gurgling. Mary Anne said, "It won't be too long now."

Tony asked, "What are we talking about here, minutes, hours, days, weeks?"

"Only God knows."

Tony pressed her, "Ballpark it for me."

"Let me put it to you this way," Mary Anne replied. "You probably have time to boil a three-minute egg but not enough time to wait for an egg to hatch."

Tony smiled and said, "So it's like Mom used to say when she was talking about someone who was very sick.' Scratch green bananas off the shopping list,' right?"

Mary Anne and Tony talked for hours about the events that just occurred, about our family, and how the many pieces of "Mom's puzzle" seemed to fall into place. One thing they discussed was how they were all able to stand next to Mom's bed when none had more than just a couple of hours sleep since Sunday and very little food. They had the sense they were channeling, and being supported by, some power outside of themselves and that perhaps the relatives that Mom was seeing were also helping them. I guess I can tell them now. We were.

As they sat next to my mom's bed, Mary Anne told Tony the story about when Sara Pieszak was diagnosed with leukemia. She told him how she and Sandra (Crea) Pieszak became reunited with their old high school friend Mary Tederous. Mary had been a nurse at Roswell Park Cancer Institute and was now a doctor. She told me that Sara called her mother Sandra while the three of them were having lunch to say she was in the doctor's office because she wasn't feeling well. Sandra called Mary Anne the next morning and said Sara was admitted to Roswell Park Cancer Institute. Mary Anne and Mary Tederous immediately headed to the hospital. They met Sandra outside of Sara's room. Mary Anne saw Sara was having difficulty breathing. She pointed at Sara, and Mary Tederous turned and knew exactly what to do and where the equipment was to save Sara's life. Mary Anne and Mary hooked up the equipment and Sandra ran to get Sara's doctor. When Sara was stable, she was sent to a room on the fifth floor. Mary Anne remembered that another cousin, Tara Nasca (Aunt Mary Nasca's granddaughter), worked at Roswell Park. Mary Anne called Aunt Mary Nasca and discovered Tara worked on the fifth floor and she would be one of the nurses caring for Sara. Knowing their dear friend Mary Tederous and Cousin Tara Nasca would be close by gave Sandra and Mary Anne a great sense of relief.

As soon as Mary Anne finished her story, a nurse walked into Mom's room and asked if they needed anything. Mary Anne said, "No, thank you."

The nurse then said, "If you need anything, just call me. My name is Sara and the other nurse on duty tonight is Tara." The coincidence was eerie.

On Thursday morning, September 24, 2009, with Mary Anne and Tony by her side, Mom stopped breathing. Mary Anne said, "That was her last breath. Write this down: 4:18 a.m." They stood there for a moment and then Mom gasped one more time. This made Tony say, "OK, Mom, now you are just messin' with us." Mom and I just looked down from heaven and smiled.

Mary Anne said, "Write down 4:20 a.m." Mary Anne and Tony stayed with Mom for five more minutes alone before calling Nurse Sara. They straightened the bed and made her look comfortable. They called Dad and told him Mom was gone. Aunt Mary, Dad, and Annette quickly came to the hospital. Frank stayed with his daughters at Aunt Mary's house so they wouldn't wake up alone in a strange house. Tearful and saddened, but also joyful that Mom was at peace, my family waited for Mom to be transported to the morgue. Tony told Aunt Mary, "You have always been like a second mother to us. Today you just got a promotion." We all wanted Aunt Mary to know how much we love and appreciate her.

My father walked up to my mother, gently touched her hand and said, "See you later, Babe."

Chapter 14:

Are All These People Related to Us?

So at seven in the morning, my family left Brooks Memorial Hospital for the last time. They left the hospital with a mixture of emotions and feelings. They felt lost, shocked, stunned, calm, amazed, saddened, tearful, joyful, proud, filled, emptied, relieved, and at peace. They didn't know whether to cry or smile. Mom's last email to them had her final instructions. She ended it with, "Now go out and celebrate." So they decided to honor her wishes by going to breakfast. They all stopped at the hotel to help get Steve ready then made the short ride to Bob Evan Restaurant in Dunkirk to celebrate Mom's life.

News spreads fast in a little town like Dunkirk. In the restaurant were many people who knew my father and Aunt Mary. They came up to express their sympathy and share stories. As the restaurant began to fill with its normal breakfast crowd, more and more people come over to our table to pay their respects to my father. My nieces and nephews were surprised to see how many people kept coming over to our table. Stephanie finally asked, "Are we related to all these people?"

Her dad told them, "Most of these people have lived in Dunkirk their whole life and know Grandma, Grandpa, and Aunt Mary. The majority of the people who came to the hospital were family, but you haven't seen anything yet. Wait until you see how many people come to the viewing and the funeral."

"How big is our family?" Nick asked.

"It's huge," said Steve, addressing his nieces and nephews. "I'll bet more than six hundred people come to the viewing and a large majority of them will be family. Every one of them knows your names and something about you. So don't be shocked when a bunch of people you have never seen hugs you and asks you about something that happened in your life. You think word travels fast on the Internet and Facebook? Wait until you see how fast the word travels in the Italian network."

Thursday was a day of preparation. Tony, Penny, and Mary Anne took the nieces and nephews to Home Depot to buy flowers to plant at the gravesite. Steve, Annette, and Dad went to meet with the priest at Holy Trinity church to finalize the funeral arrangements then headed over to the funeral home. Frank went to practice the eulogy before meeting Annette, Steve, and Dad at the funeral home.

At the church, Steve and the new pastor discussed the readings Mom wanted. They had a very in-depth theological conversation that highlighted the differences in philosophy between the Jesuit and Franciscan factions of the Catholic Church. They came to an agreement that made everyone happy. The priest had told Steve that the eulogy would be limited to seven minutes. When the priest excused himself to take a short phone call, Steve called Frank to tell him to cut out some parts of the eulogy. Frank being Frank said that's not going to happen but to tell the priest we agree to whatever amount of time we are allocated. When Steve said, "The quickest you have done the eulogy is thirteen minutes."

Frank just said, "Relax, Steve, tell the man what he wants to hear. Once I have the microphone, I will take however long it takes. He is not going to stop me during the funeral. It will be OK."

The funeral was scheduled for Monday morning. There would be two viewings at McGraw-Kowal funeral home on Sunday from one to three and again from six to eight.

Annette controlled most of the meeting with the funeral director. She had the clothes Mom wanted to wear, how she wanted her hair done, the items she wanted in the coffin, and the words for the obituary. The director showed them the room, where they could place Angela's collages, how to maximize the flow of people through the room, the procedures on where to meet at the church, who would be in what limos, the order of the cars for the procession to the cemetery, and the process at the grave site. We were so impressed with the thoroughness, professionalism, and compassion shown by the funeral director and staff. They made this very difficult process as smooth as possible.

We headed back to the house to meet with the rest of the family and the Crea's for dinner and be ready for the all the family and friends who would be stopping by the house with food and to pay their respects.

Back at the house, Angela was working on her collages. She decided we needed to lighten the mood at the house. Her plan was to address "The Wall" and Dewey's birthday. Every family has the wall. The wall is where the family portraits are hung. At my parents' house, the wall was in the dining room. It had the high school or college graduation pictures of my brothers and sisters, the tassels from their graduation caps, plus the latest 8x10 picture of every grandchild and great-grandchild. Annette's husband Dewey usually provides the comic relief. He has an incredible sense of humor and timing and he is a master at practical jokes. Dewey would always tease my mother over two issues. The first was that there was no picture of him on the wall. The second was that Myron, Mary Anne's husband, was her favorite son-in-law. He came to this conclusion because both Mom and Aunt Mary would accidentally call him Myron from time to time. My mother always laughed and said the wall was for her children and grandchildren.

Dewey would then quickly point out that David, Angela's husband, was on the wall. To which my mother replied it was their wedding picture that Angela had given to Mom. She would tell Dewey, "Send me your wedding picture, and we'll put it on the wall." The teasing was always in fun and all of the Crea's and Zaccari's were in on the story.

Angela decided she would take a picture of Dewey and have it blown up to an 8x10. She then made several copies of the picture and covered every picture on the wall with the new picture of Dewey. Angela knew Dewey and Annette would be the last to arrive back at the house since they were going to spend some time with Leah swimming at the hotel pool before coming over for dinner. She had also ordered a birthday cake with the words "Happy Birthday Myr—" and a big X through the letters M-Y-R, then the word "Dewey."

Food had been arriving most of the afternoon from Aunt Pauline, Aunt Mary Nasca, the Crea's, the Centner's, the Damiano's, and the Farina's. Angela told them all about the wall and cake story, so they all decided to wait and be part of the joke. Finally Annette and Dewey arrived carrying bags filled with groceries. No one said a word as Dewey walked right past the wall and into the kitchen. He came back into the dining room with his back to the wall, opening some soda bottles. Finally Leah couldn't hold it any longer and yelled, "Dad, look at the wall!" The look on his face was priceless as he saw the wall.

With the entire houseful of people roaring with laughter, he said, "Oh thanks, Carm; I had to wait for you to die before I could get on the wall." This brought more laughter. At that moment the mood changed from mourning Mom's death to celebrating her life.

There was a continuous stream of relatives and friends Thursday, Friday, and Saturday. The house was filled with laughter and stories. Mom would have loved it.

Karen, being the newest member of the family, was curious to learn more of the family stories. She asked Tony and Steve, "You guys always laugh and make jokes about Uncle Frank's temper. I've only met him at the wedding and the last couple days, and he is so nice. What's the story?"

Steve laughed and told her, "Frank's the oldest and his job was to protect us—and he took his job very serious. He was a pretty good athlete. Although he was not very big, he was tough. If anyone gave us any crap, Frank would jump in and either persuade them to move on or kick their ass. There was one time when the "wannabe" neighborhood tough guy was giving Annette, Tony, and me a hard time. The three of us were standing on the sidewalk ready to fight with this bully. So as he and his friends start walking toward us, Frank walked out on our porch behind us and shook his fist and stared them down. When they turned and left, the three of us started to call them babies and chickens thinking we had scared them off. Then we turned around and saw Frank going back into the house and realized it was Frank that scared them away."

Tony added, "I remember being at one of our relative's house where they had a tire swing hanging from the branch of a tree. The tire had fallen off so we were just swinging on the rope. I misjudged my jump onto the rope and was heading right for the tree. Frank ran between the tree and me and got crushed so I wouldn't get hurt. It seemed like whenever we were afraid he was always there to make sure we were OK. Like when Mom had cancer, or when Steve got hurt, or when Bobby died. He always seems to know what to do or say."

Mary Anne added, "Frank is very good in a crisis. He is not afraid to take control of a situation. He has tremendous confidence and can tell great stories to get people to believe in his vision. Plus he has this glare with his eyes that is extremely intimidating. All of that helped him become a corporate CEO."

"So are you guys talking about my dad?" asked Stephanie. "Sara and I want to hear these stories."

Tony continued, "Your dad use to babysit us frequently. To keep us entertained, he used to tell us stories. Like when the moon would rise at night, it looked like it came right out of Lake Erie. So he told us he once got into Uncle Joe's rowboat and rowed out to the edge of the lake and waited for the moon to rise up over the lake. He said that he jumped on and rode the moon up into the sky.

When we asked how he got down, he just said he dove into the lake."

Annette, hearing the story, started to laugh and said, "I believed that story for years. Did you tell them about the eyes? One time I was sitting in the bleachers at a baseball game and Frank was the umpire. This guy that I liked came over and sat by me. Between innings Frank walked toward the bleachers and looked at the guy with that glare he has and the guy says to me, 'Oh, is that your brother Frank?' When I said yes, the guy said, 'Oh, I'm sorry. I didn't know he was your brother,' and left."

Sara laughed and said, "He scared the guy away by just looking at him?"

"Yeah Sara, he has scared some guys away that I wanted to go out with by just looking at them," Stephanie added.

Tony finally said, "The best Frank story was when Stephanie was about three years old. They were visiting us here in Dunkirk and Frank was telling us about a trip he took to some exotic country. He was telling us what he ate, who he met, and what he did. We were all very impressed and interested. He had not lost his ability to tell a good story. Then Stephanie came up to him and touched him on the sleeve. She told him that Sesame Street was on TV and it was Bert and Ernie, his favorite. Frank got up and went to the TV to share that moment with his daughter. I remember how important that made you feel, Stephanie.

We all understood exactly how you felt because he has been making us feel that way our whole life."

"So where is this temper?" asked Karen.

Frank said from the next room, "Don't believe everything you hear, Karen."

Chapter 15:

The Italian Stigma

"The Italians didn't create cooking; they made it an art.
They didn't invent the arts; they honored
it like a sacrament.
They didn't discover music; they created operas and arias.
They didn't start crime; they organized it."
—Anthony Zaccari

It is troublesome that the culture that gave the world Leonardo DaVinci, Michelangelo, Dante Alighieri (author of The Divine Comedy), Galileo, Guglielmo Marconi (inventor of the radio), Enrico Fermi (who split the atom which lead to the discovered of nuclear fission), Thomas Aquinas, explorers Amerigo Vespucci, John Cabot, and Christopher Columbus, Filippo Mazzei (who whispered to Thomas Jefferson, "It is self-evident that all men are created equal"), Puccini (composer of La Boheme), Verdi (composer of the opera Rigoletto), opera singers Enrico Caruso, Mario Lanza, and Luciano Pavarotti, and not to mention Academy Award-winner

Sophia Loren, is so closely associated to organized crime and now *Jersey Shore*.

I am not complaining or crying prejudice but just making that observation. It is true that notorious criminals like Al Capone were Italian. He captured the imagination of people at that time and inspired an almost romantic and glamorous picture of Italian life. While the vast majority of Italians are honest, hardworking, God-fearing people trying to live the American dream, the topic of organized crime will surely come up in causal conversation about Italians. Let me give you an example that happened to my brother Tony. He had moved to Buffalo to start college and started dating a nice young lady whose parents were Irish. One night when he went to pick up his date, he had a conversation with her mother, a college-educated, middle-aged woman. The mother knew Tony was from Dunkirk, a city where there is a murder about once a decade. When a major crime occurs in Dunkirk, it makes the local news in Buffalo. Well it just so happened there had recently been a murder in Dunkirk. The mother asked Tony, "Did you know that kid who killed that lady?"

Tony said, "Yes, I went to school with him."

She snapped right back, "I knew it! All of you 'Eye Talians' are murderers! I will certainly not allow my daughter to go out with the likes of you people." The woman was serious. My brother was shocked.

The Italian Stigma

He explained to her that not all Italians are killers: "As a matter of fact," he said, "that kid isn't Italian. He is Puerto Rican. And not all Puerto Ricans are murderers either. Just like all Irish aren't drunks." Tony walked out of the house and could hear the mother and daughter arguing as he walked to his car.

The organized crime stigma has followed Italian Americans since the very first one arrived at Ellis Island. To paraphrase Tommy Lasorda, the long-time manager of the Los Angeles Dodgers, once said during a television interview, "Every successful Italian American has heard the whispers that their success is in some way tied to organized crime. This slur is as insulting to Italian Americans as the N word to African Americans and F word to the gay and lesbian community."

My brother Frank worked actively and aggressively to help Barack Obama become President of the United States. Frank was elated when it was announced that candidate Obama was going to become President Obama. He told his daughters, "This is such an amazing moment in American history. I never thought I would live to see this country elect a black man President. Hopefully this will be the start of a more tolerant and less divisive country."

His daughter Sara, who was just in junior high school at the time, asked, "Has an Italian ever been elected President?"

Frank sadly answered, "No."

This led Sara to ask, "Do you think it's because people would say or think or believe an Italian candidate was in the Mafia?"

"I am sure that topic would come up. I am happy this country elected an African American President, but I am sad no Italian has been given that opportunity."

So as all of our Italian relatives and friends came by the house on Friday, and Saturday while we waited for the Sunday viewing, the subject of organized crime did come up. All of my nieces and nephews were playing cards with Tony and Mary Anne. My niece Nicole asked Tony, "Has any member of our family ever been involved with organized crime?"

Tony told them all, "No. There were people in the neighborhood who were involved, but no one in our family crossed that line."

Nick asked, "Were there people trying to recruit you?"

Mary Anne answered, "You watch too many movies. Yes there were people that were involved in illegal activities, but there weren't people hanging out on the corners saying, 'Hey, kid, do you want to join an organized crime family?'"

Tony continued, "There was a story about my Grandpa Zaccari. During the depression he had bought some fruit at a very good price from a man who had set up a fruit stand. He was happy as he walked home knowing the family would have fresh fruit for a few days. On the way home, he meets his sister Stella and tells her about the fruit stand. Stella told him, 'Tony, that man and some of his friends stole that fruit from the farmers market.' Upon hearing this news, my grandfather immediately threw all the fruit into the trash. He would not have any involvement with anyone or anything that was remotely connected to organized crime. He would go without something he needed or wanted rather than have any association with a criminal. My grandfather and your grandfather exemplify our family motto—Life with Integrity."

Sara said, "There are people at my school that think my dad is in organized crime. They told me, 'Your dad is always available to take you to places and pick you up. Our parents all have jobs they have to be at every day, but your dad never seems to have to be at work.' I told them he owns his business and he has people who stay in the office. He goes out and meets people and sells insurance. Then they tell me, 'Yeah, we heard about how he came into Elk Grove and took over this guy's business. Your dad just pushed him out.'"

Mary Anne said, "Really? There are people who actually say those things?"

"Yeah, I hear it all the time. I tell them he bought the business from a friend who had to retire because of a disability."

Stephanie added, "I used to hear things like that, too. It made me so mad. I would tell them just because we are Italian; you morons think we are involved with organized crime! My dad was a corporate CEO and we moved here to buy an insurance agency so he wouldn't have to travel every week. He makes time to pick us up and get us to where we need to be."

Tony said, "Let me tell you another story Frank told me. He was about six or seven and Mass had just ended. All the people were outside the church talking and visiting. Frank was running around with another little boy. The other boy sees his grandfather, who was rumored to be in the Mafia, and they both run up to the man. The other little boy asks his grandfather for some money so they can buy something at the store next to the church. The grandfather gives them both a quarter. Now this shocks your Uncle Frank because the most we ever got from our parents for candy was maybe a nickel. The other boy and Frank start to run to the store. My Grandmother Zaccari saw what happened and called Frank to come over to her. She asked Frank, 'What did that man give you?' Frank's eyes lit up and he showed her the quarter.

"Grandma said, 'Here, give me that quarter and I will give you another one.' Frank thought that was weird, but he still had a quarter, so he was happy. Before he ran to the store, he watched Grandma walk over to the man and say to him, 'Keep your dirty money away from my Grandson,' and then she flicked the quarter in his face. Frank looked at the quarter Grandma had given him and thought, 'This one isn't any cleaner than the other one.' It was several years later when Frank understood that the man was involved with organized crime and that Grandma made sure that man knew her grandchildren were off-limits. People of every race, color, and creed are involved in illegal activities. It is a choice to cross the line and commit a crime. It is not something that happens to you because your last name ends in a vowel.

"Your grandmother used to tell us all the time, 'If people put as much effort and energy into their job as they do trying to get away with something, they would be very successful without resorting to crime.'"

My nephew Chris added, "We all have to remember one thing: 'Life with Integrity.'

Chapter 16:

Yes, All These People Are Related to Us

Sunday morning, Angela and David brought the collages to the funeral home. Angela did an amazing job; the pictures were sure to stir up many good memories for all the visitors. The first viewing was at 1:00 p.m. It didn't take long for hundreds of people to arrive. My family formed two lines one on each side of the coffin to greet our family and friends. Mary Anne, Dad, Annette, and Steve were in the line leading to the coffin. Frank, Tony, Penny, and Frank's daughters were on the side leading away from the coffin. Since Frank had moved away from the area nearly forty years ago, Tony and Penny stood near him so they could tell him the names of all the people. It was like the scene from the movie *American President,* where the secretary stands near Michael Douglas and tells him the names of the White House staff so he can address each staff member by name. As people left the coffin and walked toward Frank, Tony would lean in and whisper, "Russell Mancuso," or "Rae Lynn," and so on. Frank, in turn, greeted each person by name, gave them a hug, and thanked them for coming. Stephanie and Sara were shocked by the number of people and even more shocked that every person knew who they were. Four hundred people came to the first viewing. My nieces and nephews heard many wonderful stories about their grandmother. Stories like how Mom and Dad would make meals and deliver them to families in need. How she would bring struggling families dishes, pots, pans, clothes, or winter coats. How she would drive elderly people to and from their doctor appointments. How Mom and Aunt Mary taught young wives how to bake bread and how to grow vegetables in an area as small as a window box to save money.

At one point Stephanie said to her father, "I had no idea Grandma did so many things for so many people. She was like Mother Teresa."

Frank told Stephanie, "Your grandmother didn't stand on the sidelines and wait for someone else to act. When she saw someone in need, she did something to help. That's the way it was when we were growing up. We were surrounded by family. Everyone helped each other without being asked, because they knew the family would be there for them in their time of need. It was a great place and a great way to grow up. I often feel that you and Sara got cheated out this experience because we lived so far away. I am so happy that you were able to spend so much time with Grandma while you were in college. I am so sorry that Sara didn't get the same experience."

"Dad, Sara got to spend time with Grandma whenever we visited, which was several times a year."

"I know, but it is not the same as when you live close by."

"I know what you mean, Dad. Mom's family lived within two blocks of us, but they never did things like your family. I mean we got together for holidays and things, but it seemed more like an obligation. Mom and Aunt Jennifer never seemed to be very close, and Sara and I were never close to our cousins from that side. It seemed like there were conditions that had to be met before we would be accepted."

"It's all about family, Stephanie. It is all about unconditional love. I know my family can be overbearing at times, but all we have is each other. No matter what happens to me, you and Sara have to know and believe that my father and my brothers and sisters will always be there for you. I know your mother has said things to you and Sara—that I care more about my brothers and sisters than I do about her. I hope you know that is not true. The Zaccari's and the Mancuso's accept and unconditionally love every person in our family. I hope you saw that this week. I hope you saw that every person who came to see Grandma this week truly cares about you and Sara even though you never met most of them. Every one of these people will do whatever they can to help you. That's what family is about. It's like Annette said the first night, when one of us is tickled, we all laugh. When one of us is cut, we all bleed."

The first viewing ended about three o'clock. The Zaccari's and Crea's all headed back to the house, where the Centner's and Porpiglia's had brought enough food to feed a small nation. The house looked like it did for all those Christmas Eve celebrations years ago—full of family, food, and love. Everyone ate and laughed and reminisced until it was time to go back for the second viewing. Mom, Sara Pieszak, and I all smiled as we watched our family celebrate Mom's life.

The second viewing was larger than the first. Nearly five hundred people came by to pay their respects. About eight o'clock the large crowd had left. The local priest and the funeral directors came into the room for the final prayers and final moments before the coffin was closed. In the room were my father, brothers, sisters, nieces and nephews, Aunt Mary Crea, five of her six children, and several of her grandchildren. The funeral director asked my brother Frank if he wanted just the immediate family in the room. Frank said, "This is the immediate family." The priest said the series of pre-funeral prayers, and then, one by one, starting with my father, my "immediate family" walked up to the coffin and had their last private and personal moment with Mom. I felt the heartbreak with my father as he said goodbye to the only woman he ever loved, the woman who shared his life for the past fifty-seven years. I saw the deep sorrow in everyone's eyes. I saw how lost Aunt Mary looked saying goodbye to her sister and best friend of seventy-seven years. Each of my nieces and nephews put a note in the coffin with Mom.

When all the final goodbyes were said, the funeral director closed and sealed the coffin. With heavy and broken hearts, my family went to eat at Aunt Mary's house.

It was rainy and windy Monday morning, September 28, as my family headed to Holy Trinity Church. The first people waiting at the church were Uncle Joe and Aunt Ceta. Aunt Ceta hugged Dad and whispered, "Frank, I am so sorry for what happened. I should have apologized years ago and—."

My father cut her off and just said, "The peace was made. There is no more unfinished business or regrets."

The church filled quickly. There were close to three hundred people at the funeral. It was a beautiful and moving ceremony. The priest announced that my brother Frank would be delivering the eulogy. As Frank walked up to the altar, the rain seemed to turn to hail, which pounded on the skylight of the church. Sara leaned toward her sister and cousins and whispered, "I don't think God is too happy about Dad going up there." This brought a chuckle from the family and helped to ease the sadness.

Chapter 17:

The Eulogy

"On behalf of my Father, thank you for your tremendous outpouring of love and support. After Mass there will be a graveside service at St. Joseph's cemetery, followed by a brunch about 1:15 at the Moose Club. After all, what is a Zaccari celebration without food? Please come and share this time with us.

"In your program is a quote from a wise person. It says, 'The loss of your mother is the first sorrow wept alone.' We, her children and grandchildren, feel the full measure of those words today as we all gather to honor our mother and celebrate her life."

"Carmela 'no middle name' Mancuso Zaccari was born March 8, 1932. She was the twelfth of twelve children. When you have that many children, beds are at a premium. So our mother's first bed was a macaroni box. You old Italians know what I am talking about."

"I once asked my grandmother why she didn't give mom a middle name—and as only Grandma Mancuso could say with that get-the-hell-out-of-here wave of her hand, 'When you have that many children, you run out of names to use.'"

"Mom married Frank Zaccari fifty-seven years ago at Holy Trinity Church. Father Bernardo performed the service. (You didn't think you could come into *this* church and not hear at least one reference to Father Bernardo did you?) In this church community, their children were baptized and confirmed. Together, under some very adverse conditions, my parents created a legacy of love, determination, and service to their God, family, and friends."

"My mother wore many hats. She was the mother of five children in eight years. Try doing that! She was a two-time cancer survivor. The first time, she was diagnosed with colon cancer in 1967. She was also pregnant. In 1967 no one in medical history had ever survived this combination. While we all prayed for the best, we prepared for the worst. But God had plans for our mother, and he let her know during the surgery. My mother never spoke of this experience; fearing people would think she had lost her mind. But what happened is an event similar to the popular book *90 Minutes in Heaven*. During her surgery, mom felt she was drawn to a brilliant light. She spoke to a beautiful voice that told her not to be afraid. This voice was very calm and reassuring. My mother asked if she was going to die. She was told, 'Not yet, not at this time.' She asked why our beloved cousin Bobby Farina survived a car crash only to die the following year in a plane crash. She was told, 'Everything happens for a reason. It all fits together like a puzzle. Every grain of sand, every hair on your head has a purpose. You will understand later.' I think she understands it now."

"Now there are those who will say this conversation did not occur. They will say it was the effect of anesthesia or the operating room lights. But I choose to believe that God met with my mother that day to let her know that, though He had prepared a place for her, she had more to do on earth. And boy did she do a lot."

"Anyone who came in contact with my mother knew they had just met an extraordinary woman. My parents' house became an oasis for love and peace. Anyone who came to the house became family. They were loved without conditions. You also received a nice side benefit in that she fed all of you very well. My Aunt Lucy once said that walking into my parents' home was like walking into a little piece of heaven.

"My mother never graduated from high school. She dropped out to help support her family after Grandma Mancuso was injured and could not work. She planned to go back, but life had other plans.

"For someone who didn't finish high school, education was her passion. All five of us can recall many conversations that included the phrase, 'You will graduate from college if it kills us both.' Education was so important that mom finished her GED in 1970—one year before I graduated from high school. She didn't just talk the talk.

"Five children! All college graduates, all honor students, nine college degrees between us and counting. Eight grandchildren! Three college graduates, one a PhD, three still in college, one in high school, and Leah just starting first grade. Not bad for someone who had to drop out of high school."

"It wasn't easy putting five children through Catholic schools and college. It was not without tremendous sacrifice, service, and dedication from our parents. Mom ironed altar linens for Father Bernardo for years so we could go to Holy Trinity School. Our parents worked tirelessly at every school and church event including bingo and bake sales to send us to Cardinal Mindszenty. Mom was secretary at Holy Trinity School for more than twenty years. Her love and dedication to education inspired two generations of Holy Trinity graduates—many of whom, up until her last days, warmly greeted her with a 'Hello, Mrs. Zaccari. Do you remember me?'"

"After her retirement, she continued her life of service. She was completely devoted to her grandchildren: Angela, Christopher, Nicole, Nick, Stephanie, Cherish, Sara, Leah, and her great-grandson Ethan. Everything stopped whenever anyone of them was around. They loved being around her as much as she loved spending precious time with each one. The bond was special. Grandma spoke of each of you with great joy and pride. There are many women who become a grandmother. There are only a select few who earn the title of Grandma.

"We cannot forget to mention that our family grew to include loving and supportive spouses; Diana and Penny, beautiful wives and loving mothers; Myron, mom's favorite son-in-law, in New York, and Dewey, her other favorite son-in-law, in Arizona. And we welcome our most recent additions David and Karen, whom Mom loved as much as her own grandchildren.

"Now after seventy-seven years of service and dedication, mom is enjoying the reward that God promised her back in 1967.

"Close your eyes and picture in your mind this reunion at heaven's gate:

"Her baby who died during the surgery is up front, jumping with excitement. Sara Pieszak is there with Grandma and Grandpa Mancuso. I see Aunt Grace and Aunt Lucy and her other brothers and sisters. Uncle Phil and Uncle Carl are there with Grandpa Zaccari. Aunt Nina has Bobby and Uncle Al running around planting roses, and if you listen—if you really listen—you can hear Grandma Zaccari yelling at Uncle Pete to get her to the gate two hours early so she can get a good seat. Some things never change. It must be an amazing celebration and with all those Italians, just imagine the food!

"To all of you here today who joined us in our celebration of our mother's life, we thank you for your love and support. Special thanks to our second mother, Aunt Mary Crea, who never left our sides as we said our goodbyes.

"In remembrance of our mother, I would like to close with these simple words of wisdom that she was so fond of:

When you remember me…
Remember me laughing—not crying
Remember me singing—not sighing
Remember me living—not dying
Or don't remember me at all.

"That, Mom, is how you will be remembered as we hold you in our hearts…forever."

Chapter 18:

The Final Resting Place

After the funeral Mass, a very long car procession made its way from Holy Trinity Church to St. Joseph's Cemetery. As the hearse parked at the chapel, the sun came out for the first time. I know it was a message from God that Mom was comfortable and watching out for everyone from heaven.

Mom was laid to rest at the family plot her father had purchased in 1913. As the baby of the family, she was Grandpa Mancuso's favorite. It was fitting that Mom was placed next to her father. My father will take the plot on her other side.

The reception at the Moose Lodge was the final step. Over one hundred friends and family members spent the rest of the afternoon laughing and catching up. The finality started to set in as my family left the reception. In the morning, Frank and his family would be flying back to California. Annette and Steve would stay another few days before flying back to Phoenix. Slowly over the next few days, everyone returned to their day-to-day life, but that life would never be the same.

My work was far from done, but now I have Mom to help. Our first task occurred forty-five days after the funeral. We were there to help Frank, Stephanie, and Sara pick up the pieces after Diana left the family. I recall Mom's last words to Stephanie and Sara were, "Stay close to your father; listen to your father," like she knew what was coming.

Two months after the funeral, my father was home alone cleaning up after he ate lunch. While in the kitchen, he had a sense that someone was in the house. He walked through the dining room into the living room, but he saw nothing. He looked in the room where Mom slept when she was too weak to walk upstairs. In the silence of the big empty house, he believed he heard muffled voices but was not able to find anybody. As he walked back into the kitchen, he again felt the presence of another person in the house. He saw a shadow move on the wall in the dining room. He walked back into the dining room, but again he saw no one or anything that would explain the shadow. He wondered if his mind was playing tricks on him. He thought maybe someone was on the porch. He walked out the front door. The street was unusually empty; he walked around the house, but did not see or hear anyone. He shrugged his shoulders and headed back into the house. A few moments later, he heard people talking. Then he heard the sound of someone laughing from upstairs.

He walked upstairs and looked into every room. Again, the rooms were empty, quiet, and undisturbed. He walked back into the dining room and looked at the picture of Mom and said, "Hey, as long as you are here, you might as well help clean up." He laughed. Mom and I laughed, too.

Chapter 19:

A Grandmother's Memories

My mother kept a journal that contains funny stories and memories of her grandchildren. I hope your grandmother has such a journal. The memories are priceless.

My three year old grandson Christopher and I were walking in the backyard when I notice the flowers had been trampled. I said to him, "Chris it looks like someone stepped on our flowers." He said, "Grandpa stepped on the Fod Duse."

When Sara was about four, she called the dog to come into the house in a voice loud enough for the neighbors to hear, "Get in here, you goddamn dog!" When everyone looked at her, startled, she calmly said, "That's how my Dad calls the dog."

Sara called me one time when her mother was making fudge. When I asked her what she was doing she said, "I'm eating smudge."

Cherish sang in her Christmas pageant, "Angels We Have Heard on High." Her words were "Gloria…In egg shells and day old." During the same pageant, the class sang, "We Three Kings of Orient Are…." Cherish sang, "We Three Kings had trouble so far."

Once time during Mass, just before the communion where everyone says, "Lord, I am not worthy to receive you, but say the word and I shall be healed." Cherish asked her mom, "What's the word?"

When Nick was afraid of the lightening, he came to me. Each time I assured him we were safe in the house, since his father had the house grounded. Nick's reply was, "Why did he ground the house, Grandma? Did it do something bad?"

My daughter Annette traveled to China to adopt my precious little China doll, Leah. One day she saw a pregnant woman and asked her, "What is in your belly?" When the woman said, "I am going to have a baby." Leah asked, "Are you going to China?"

When Sara was taking dance classes, she decided she didn't want to dance. When Frank asked her why she didn't dance she said, "When they play music I like, then I'll dance."

I was watching Angela and Dave with Ethan. They are so good with him. They are so patient. You really can see the difference between young parents and more mature parents. Ethan is such a good little boy. He's always happy.

When Chris was about three years old, he would measure a Popsicle he was eating with the one his grandfather or I were eating. If ours were bigger, then he would take the larger piece for himself. My husband loved this. He would just hold his half of the Popsicle, and Chris would trade several times. His mother wasn't too crazy about this, but we told her, "We're his grandparents; it's our job to spoil him."

At age four or five, when playing a game with Chris, he would always announce, "I will win this game!" And when he cheated, he would say, "I make up the rules as we go along."

At Steffi's dance recital in 1999, Frank was so moved by his beautiful daughter's performance, that he had tears in his eyes. Sara went to Annette and said, "Parina [Godmother], my Dad is crying, and I didn't even do anything!"

In closing, my family hopes that you saw many things about your family in this book. We hope it made you smile. Friends and acquaintances come and go, but family…family is forever. Thank you for allowing us to share our story.

Inside the Spaghetti Bowl

Zaccari Family Crest

The Zaccari Coat of Arms

The Zaccari Coat of Arms was registered around 1977. Let me try my best to explain it to you. In the upper left-hand corner is a picture of a mountain goat or ram called a Zack or something that sounds like Zaccari in the Greek language. Apparently the Zaccari's were originally from Greece where they might have been herders, (or maybe they looked like or smelled like a goat), no one knows for sure.

The picture in the upper right-hand corner is to show how they struggled, represented by the sword, to cross the Adriatic Sea to come to Italy from Greece.

My Grandfather came to America with his three sisters who are symbolized in the bottom left-hand corner picture:

Stella, depicted here as the star married a man named Vito Damiano and they had several children.

The rose represents my Great Aunt Rose who married Frank Flagella who also had many children.

The oil lamp is supposed to be Jenny. In Italian her name is Giovanna which is the word for oil, I think. Jenny married Frank Crea. They had four children.

The person talking to the fish is St. Anthony of Padua (it is said that St. Anthony was a very eloquent speaker that even the fish would come to the surface to hear him) represents my Grandfather Anthony Zaccari. He married Jenny Saglimben and they had five children.

The last picture on the crest is how the family grew from humble beginnings. I remember someone saying that the drops of blood represent the members who married into the family and contributed to the growth of the family. Like rain to a tree, the members who married into the family are essential to its growth.

My Grandfather Anthony Zaccari was known for his integrity. Integrity, doing what is right because and only because it is the right thing to do. So across the bottom of the coat of arms is the family motto; **"LIFE WITH INTEGRITY."**

And that is exactly what it means, Life with integrity. No exceptions, no excuses.

Made in the USA
Middletown, DE
08 February 2020